CW01429201

NEW YORK TRAVEL GUIDE 2025

DISCOVER TOP ATTRACTIONS, INSIDER TIPS, AND SMART BUDGETING FOR FIRST-TIME AND RETURNING VISITORS

ELI STATEN

New York Travel Guide 2025

Copyright © 2025 by Eli Staten

All rights reserved.

No part of this book may be reproduced, distributed, or transmitted in any form or by any means, including photocopying, recording, or other electronic or mechanical methods, without the prior written permission of the publisher, except in the case of brief quotations embodied in critical reviews and certain other noncommercial uses permitted by copyright law. For permission requests, please contact the publisher at the address below.

Disclaimer : Eli Staten

The information in this book, *New York Travel Guide 2025*, is based on extensive research, personal experiences, and publicly available sources. Every effort has been made to ensure that the details provided are accurate and up-to-date at the time of publication. However, the author makes no warranties or guarantees, express or implied, about the completeness, accuracy, reliability, or suitability of the information contained in this book for any particular purpose.

The content is intended for general information and guidance purposes only. The author is not responsible for any changes in conditions, schedules, services, prices, or availability, nor for any loss, injury, inconvenience, or damage that may arise from reliance on the information provided.

Readers are encouraged to independently verify details such as business hours, prices, and locations before making travel arrangements. The author assumes no liability or responsibility for any errors, omissions, or changes in the content of this guide. Any reliance placed on the information is strictly at the reader's own risk.

CONTENTS

INTRODUCTION

When you first step off the plane, you'll feel it—the energy that's unlike anywhere else. The moment you leave the airport, whether it's JFK, LaGuardia, or Newark, you're not just visiting a city; you're walking into something alive. You'll notice the air smells different, almost electric, buzzing with life as taxis rush past and crowds move like they've been doing this all their lives, which they have. It's an experience that can feel overwhelming at first, but give it a few hours, and you'll find yourself moving right along with it.

Where is this place? Well, geographically speaking, it's on the northeastern coast of the United States, tucked between the Atlantic Ocean and the Hudson River, but that hardly explains the feeling of being here. History built this city, starting with the Dutch in the 1600s, when it was called New Amsterdam. Now, centuries later, it's one of the most powerful cities in the world. But you don't need a history lesson to feel the weight of its past; you can sense it in every building, every street, every tiny deli where you stop to grab a bagel. It's everywhere.

Timing your visit is crucial. I've been there in the dead heat of summer, sweating through my shirt as I walked through Central Park, and I've been there in the biting cold of winter, sipping hot chocolate while watching ice skaters twirl at Rockefeller Center. The city changes dramatically with the seasons, and each has its own charm. If you prefer mild weather and fewer crowds, spring and fall are your best bets. The air is crisp, especially in autumn, and you'll want to spend hours walking, just soaking in the vibrant colors of the leaves in the park or on the tree-lined streets of Brooklyn. But even in winter, despite the cold, there's something magical about the city around the holidays. The lights, the massive Christmas trees, the whole place feels like a scene out of a movie.

Expect to see a lot of people. With around **60 million visitors a year**, you'll notice the crowds in places like Times Square, which always feels like it's bursting at the seams. But that's the beauty of this place: it's never empty, and it's constantly alive. I remember standing on the Brooklyn Bridge once, looking back at the skyline just as the sun set. There were people everywhere, taking photos, walking dogs, or just standing in awe of the view. That's the thing—no matter where you go, you're always part of a bigger scene, part of the story that's unfolding in the city around you.

Budgeting your trip doesn't have to be scary. I've done it both ways: once, I splurged on a hotel right in Midtown, steps from Broadway and the bustling streets, and another time, I stayed in a cozy Airbnb in Brooklyn, paying half the price and getting a quieter, more local experience. You don't need to break the bank to enjoy this city. You can grab a slice of pizza for a few dollars or sit down for an extravagant meal at a high-end restaurant if that's more your style.

A

lot depends on how you want to experience the city. You can easily spend between **$200 to $400 a day** if you're aiming for a middle ground—decent accommodation, solid meals, a show or two, maybe a few subway rides. But if you're savvy, you can cut that down. **The secret is finding balance.** One day you might splurge on a nice dinner in the West Village, and the next, you're grabbing bagels from a local deli and enjoying a picnic in Central Park. That's the beauty of it here—there's no one way to experience the city, and you can shape it based on your budget and mood.

Getting around the city is a breeze once you've figured out the subway, and trust me, after a day or two, you'll feel like a pro. The first time I rode the subway, I was completely confused by the express trains, but now I love how fast and efficient it is. **Buy yourself a MetroCard, and don't be afraid to ask someone for directions**—locals are in a hurry, but they're helpful if you ask quickly and respectfully. Walking is also one of the best ways to explore. I've found some of my favorite spots just by wandering without a plan—like stumbling upon a tiny bookstore in the East Village or a hidden rooftop bar in Chinatown that felt like a secret just waiting to be discovered.

You might be wondering if **what you've seen online matches the real experience**. To a degree, yes. The **bright lights of Times Square**, the **iconic yellow taxis** racing by, the **skyscrapers that make you feel small**—that's all real. But there's something much deeper here that photos and videos can't capture. For example, everyone knows about the Statue of Liberty and the Empire State Building, but not as many people talk about the feeling of walking through the quiet, tree-lined streets of the West Village at dusk or sitting in Washington Square Park, watching street performers while the arch frames the view of the city behind you. It's these moments—the ones you don't plan for—that will make you fall in love with this place.

New York is different from other cities, and you'll feel that as soon as you arrive. There's a rhythm to life here, a kind of buzz that you don't get in quieter, slower-paced places. I've been to many cities, but there's something about this one that's always moving, always changing. Even when you think you've seen it all, you'll discover something new—a tiny restaurant tucked away in the Lower East Side or a mural in Bushwick that wasn't there the last time you visited. **You don't visit this city; you experience it.**

You might hear that it's an overwhelming place, but honestly, after a day or two, **you start to fall into the rhythm.** Sure, the crowds in Midtown can be thick, and the subway at rush hour is an experience all its own, but there's a sense of excitement in all of that. You'll find yourself weaving through the streets like a local in no time, grabbing coffee on the go, and mastering the art of walking fast without bumping into people.

One of my favorite memories is walking the High Line in early fall. The air was cool but not too cold, and the path wasn't crowded. You're above the streets, surrounded by gardens, with the Hudson River on one side and the city's buildings on the other. It's one of those places where the city feels different—calmer, somehow—and it reminds you that there are so many layers to this place.

That's the real magic—no matter how much you plan or how many lists of top attractions you follow, the best parts of the city are often the ones you stumble upon by accident.

The city is easier than you think, even though it might feel overwhelming at first glance. **The subway is your best friend** when it comes to navigating the different boroughs. It runs 24/7, so no matter what time it is, you'll always have a way to get where you need to go. That weekly **MetroCard for $34** will save you a ton of money, especially if you're planning to move around a lot. The thing is, the subway may seem confusing with its endless lines and stations, but after a couple of rides, you'll get the hang of it. Just follow the signs, and don't hesitate to ask someone if you're unsure—you'd be surprised how helpful New Yorkers can be once you break through the hustle. Plus, walking is a huge part of the experience here. The city is best seen on foot, where you can stumble upon random street performers in the subway stations or tiny, hidden cafes tucked between buildings.

It's funny how the images you see online, or in movies, always focus on the big, flashy parts of the city, but **the real magic is in the details you don't see.** Sure, **Times Square** is just as loud, bright, and busy as it looks on screen, and the skyline really does stretch out in a breathtaking display. But those aren't the moments you'll remember most. It's the quiet morning walks through Central Park, where the city feels like it's just waking up, or standing on the edge of the Brooklyn Heights Promenade, looking back at Manhattan as the sun sets, painting the sky in colors you didn't expect.

I once walked through **Greenwich Village** on a lazy Sunday afternoon and ended up at a tiny bookstore I'd never heard of, filled with rare and used books that had their own history. It wasn't on any tourist guide or list I'd seen online, but it felt like discovering something meant just for me. **That's what this city does**—It's the unpredictability that makes it special, really. One moment, you might be weaving through the crowded streets of Midtown, caught in the middle of the hustle, and the next, you could find yourself in a quiet neighborhood like **Brooklyn Heights**, where the brownstone buildings and tree-lined streets make you forget you're in one of the busiest cities in the world. That's the thing—you never quite know what the city is going to show you next.

You could be on your way to see one of the big tourist spots, but then you spot a tiny restaurant or a corner café that pulls you in, and before you know it, you're sitting with a fresh bagel or a slice of pizza, chatting with a local, feeling like you've stumbled on your own private slice of the city. **The best parts of this city are often unplanned.** It's in those little moments where you let go of the map and just wander. That's when you really start to get what makes this place different. It's not just about the big, iconic landmarks—though those are spectacular in their own right—but about **how the city reveals itself to you** in these smaller, more intimate ways.

For example, I once spent an afternoon just walking along the **High Line**, a park built on an old elevated railway that runs through the West Side. The gardens are beautiful, and the views of the Hudson River on one side and the city skyline on the other are incredible. But what really struck me was the feeling of peace up there, high above the chaos of the streets. It felt like a secret escape, and yet it's one of the most popular attractions. That's the duality of this city—it can feel both massive and personal, busy and quiet, all at once.

The cost of a trip can vary widely depending on how you want to experience it. You can spend hundreds on a fancy dinner or keep it simple with a couple of slices from a pizza joint that's been serving locals for decades. Either way, you'll get something unforgettable. **A $3 slice** from a local pizzeria can be as satisfying as a meal at a Michelin-starred restaurant, because **it's not about the price here—it's about the experience.** You'll find that some of the most memorable moments won't cost you anything. Walking through the **Metropolitan Museum of Art** on a pay-what-you-wish day, or just sitting by the Bethesda Fountain in Central Park, watching the city go by—it's all part of the fabric of the city, whether you're spending big or keeping it low-key.

And then there's the diversity—**the people, the cultures, the food.** You can eat your way around the world without ever leaving the city. One night, you might have sushi from a tiny, authentic spot in the East Village, and the next morning, you're in **Chinatown**, grabbing dumplings for breakfast. There's something for everyone here, no matter what you're into. It's a city built on immigrants, and you feel that in every neighborhood. Each one has its own flavor, its own history, and you can spend days just wandering through them, soaking it all in.

I've always found that **this city feels like several cities in one.** The vibe in **Harlem** is completely different from **SoHo**, which is a world away from **Flushing in Queens** or **Staten Island's calm parks and waterfront views.** You don't just visit one version of the city; you visit many, each with its own rhythm and energy. One moment you're in a sleek, modern part of Manhattan with glass towers stretching into the sky, and the next you're in a historic corner of **The Bronx**, surrounded by music and street art that tell the story of a neighborhood's past and future.

And about that **energy**—it's real. You'll feel it everywhere, not just in the big, iconic places. You'll sense it when you're walking across the **Brooklyn Bridge** at sunset, with the skyline lighting up behind you and the river rushing below. It's there when you're watching the locals go about their day, rushing through the subway or standing at a food truck, chatting about their plans for the weekend. It's the feeling that there's always something happening, always something to do or see or taste. **The city doesn't stop**, and that's part of the magic. You can explore from early morning until late at night, and you'll barely scratch the surface.

But despite how fast it moves, **the city will also wait for you.** You don't have to rush to see it all at once. Take your time. Walk slower through **Central Park**. Sit on a bench in **Bryant Park**, and just people-watch for a while. Go ahead and grab that second cup of coffee from a local shop and relax. You'll find that even in the middle of all the noise, there are moments of quiet, spaces where the city lets you breathe.

CHAPTER 1
WELCOME TO THE CITY THAT NEVER SLEEPS

You'll notice it as soon as you set foot on the sidewalk—the way people move with purpose, the constant buzz of conversation, the never-ending stream of taxis, and the sound of a million different stories unfolding all around you. This isn't just any city; it's a place where everything happens— sometimes all at once—and you're right in the middle of it. Every street here tells a different story, whether you're wandering through the old, charming blocks of the West Village, where the buildings are low and the trees are tall, or standing in the shadows of the towering skyscrapers in Midtown, where the world seems to spin just a little faster.

The city doesn't slow down for anyone, but that's part of what makes it exciting, isn't it? Here, you're never far from something amazing, whether it's a quiet spot in Central Park that feels like a world away from the chaos, or a busy corner where the lights from Times Square make everything glow, even in the middle of the night.

Every visit is different, because this place is constantly changing. Maybe you've been here before and think you've seen it all—but you haven't, because this city never stops surprising you. You might find yourself at a gallery in Chelsea where the art is so fresh it feels like it was just finished this morning, or in a tiny restaurant in the Lower East Side where the food is so good you can't stop talking about it.

This city is built on diversity, on bringing together people from every corner of the world, each contributing something unique, something special, something that makes this place unlike anywhere else. You could spend your morning exploring the hustle of Chinatown, your afternoon wandering through the history in Harlem, and your evening soaking up the cool vibe in Williamsburg, and you'd still only scratch the surface.

It's a city of neighborhoods, each with its own pulse, its own rhythm, its own soul. The Lower East Side buzzes with the energy of the night, the East Village is a constant blend of creativity and rebellion, and then there's SoHo, where art and fashion collide in every storefront and gallery space. But it's not just about where you are—it's about who you meet, the experiences you have, and the stories you take home with you.

For the first-timer, this place can feel overwhelming, but don't worry, because that's part of the adventure. It's not about trying to do everything— it's about finding the moments that matter to you. Maybe it's standing on the Brooklyn Bridge at sunrise, watching the city wake up, or maybe it's catching a Broadway show that leaves you breathless.

And if you've been here before, you know there's always something new to discover, because this city doesn't sit still. Every corner has something different to offer, every block has its own character, and every visit gives you another chance to explore something unexpected.

This isn't just a city, it's a living, breathing thing, constantly moving, constantly growing, constantly offering new experiences for those who seek them out. Whether you're here for the first time or the fiftieth, this place has something for you, something that will stick with you long after you leave, something that will keep pulling you back, again and again.

What's New in 2025

2025 brings a wave of fresh experiences you can't miss, starting with the SkyView Observation Deck, the city's highest outdoor platform, giving you a view that's unmatched. This isn't just another tall building, it's an experience where you step onto a glass floor, look down and see the city beneath you, feeling like you're floating above the streets, and all around you, the lights and the skyline come alive in a way that's both thrilling and unforgettable. It's designed to be more than just a place to look out—it's a place where you feel connected to the energy and scale of the city in a way you haven't before, and if you're looking to understand the scale and beauty of this place in a single moment, this is where you need to be.

Food lovers, this is your year because the new Global Eats Market in

Midtown is opening, and it's like a culinary world tour in one place. You're going to find the best street food from across the globe, all within a few steps of each other. Imagine this—authentic tacos with just the right amount of spice, fresh sushi that melts in your mouth, handmade pasta that tastes like it came straight from a kitchen in Italy, and it's all made by people who are passionate about their food, who've brought the flavors of their homeland here for you to taste and enjoy. This market isn't just about eating, it's about discovering, trying something new with every bite, and if you're someone who loves food, this is going to be your go-to spot, the place where you come back again and again because there's always something different to try, always something to savor.

Art gets a new home this year with the opening of The Fusion Museum. This isn't a place where you just walk through and look at art hanging on the walls, this is where you become part of the art itself. You're going to find exhibits that mix digital art with classical pieces, performances happening right in front of you, installations that invite you to touch, move, and even create. It's interactive, it's immersive, and it's designed to make you see art in a whole new way, and if you're someone who loves being at the cutting edge of creativity, this is where you're going to spend your time, losing yourself in the process of creation and expression that's unlike anything else.

Fashion is taking over the Meatpacking area with the new Trend District. This isn't just about shopping—it's about seeing what's next in the world of style before it even hits the runway. You're going to find pop-up shops from designers who are just starting to make their mark, boutiques that are show-casing pieces you can't find anywhere else, and everything about this district is about being ahead of the curve, about wearing something that nobody else has yet, something that makes a statement. It's where fashion trends are born, where creativity and style meet, and if you want to be the first to see, the first to wear, this is where you're going to be, exploring the future of fashion.

Harbor Park is the newest green space opening up along the East River, and it's not just a park—it's where you go to escape the city while still being in the heart of it. You've got long paths perfect for biking, places to sit and just watch the water flow by, and areas where you can get out on the river with a kayak or paddleboard, seeing the skyline from a whole new angle. This is where you go when you want a break, when you need to slow down for a minute and just breathe, but you still want to be surrounded by the energy and beauty of the city.

The Eco Ferry system is launching this year, giving you a new way to get around. It's not just faster, it's green, connecting different parts of the city through the rivers with boats that are as good for the environment as they are convenient. You're going to see the city from the water, cruising along while reducing your carbon footprint, and it's a fresh, scenic, and eco-friendly way to move around, changing the way you experience this place.

2025 is the year to explore, to discover, and to see this place like you've never seen it before. Whether you're into art, food, fashion, or just want to find a new way to experience the energy of the city, this is your time to dive in, to take it all in, and to make this year the one where you see it all, experience it all, and leave with memories you won't forget. Every new attraction, every new event, every new corner you turn is going to show you something different, something that makes this year special, something that will make you want to come back again and again to see what else has changed, what else is new, and what else you can discover.

How to Use This Guide

This guide is built to be your ultimate tool, whether you're planning every detail of your trip ahead of time or just figuring things out as you go, and everything you need is right where you'd expect it to be, making it quick and simple to find what you're looking for. You're going to start by diving into the planning sections, where you'll get all the essential details lined up—things like the best times to visit, how to budget smartly so you can stretch your money further without missing out on the must-do experiences, and how to pick the perfect place to stay, whether you want luxury or something more budget-friendly.

Each neighborhood is laid out clearly, so you'll know exactly what to see, what to skip, and where to find the hidden gems that make each area unique. Whether you're in the mood to explore the trendy boutiques of SoHo, take in the culture in Harlem, or simply wander through Central Park, you'll find all the details right here, making it easy to navigate through the city and enjoy your time without any unnecessary hassle. This guide gives you specific tips on where to eat, where to shop, where to relax, and where to experience the true vibe of each neighborhood, so you're not just seeing the city—you're experiencing it like someone who knows it well.

As you move through the guide, you'll also find practical tips embedded right where you need them, like how to navigate the subway system efficiently, how to avoid the worst of the crowds at popular spots, and how to find clean, accessible restrooms when you need them. This isn't just about listing attractions—it's about giving you the information that makes your trip smoother, more enjoyable, and way more manageable, so you can focus on what matters —having a great time.

And if you're the kind of traveler who likes to figure things out on the fly, you'll love how easy it is to flip through the guide and find exactly what you need in seconds. No need to dig through pages of unrelated info—just turn to the neighborhood or section you're interested in, and you'll have all the recommendations, directions, and details you need, ready to go. Everything is designed to be clear and accessible, making it as easy as possible to get around the city and make the most of every moment.

This guide is all about making your experience as effortless as possible, so you can focus on enjoying the city rather than figuring out logistics. With everything broken down into easy-to-follow sections, you'll always have the information you need right at your fingertips, whether you're planning your next move or simply soaking up the city as you go. No fluff, no filler—just the core details that will help you navigate, explore, and truly experience everything this place has to offer, so you can get the most out of every single day you spend here.

CHAPTER 2
PLANNING YOUR NYC ADVENTURE

When to Visit: Seasonal Highlights

Spring is when you see the city truly come alive. The cherry blossoms in Central Park are a sight you won't forget, with the entire park transforming into a sea of pink and white. You'll want to spend time walking through the park, especially around the Reservoir and the Conservatory Garden, where the flowers are in full bloom and the atmosphere is calm yet vibrant. The New York **Botanical Garden** in the Bronx is another must-visit in spring, especially during the Orchid Show, where the variety of blooms is so vast and colorful that it almost feels like stepping into another world. Tribeca Film Festival is happening, and you get to see films before they hit mainstream theaters, often with the filmmakers there to give you insights into their work—it's not just watching a movie, it's experiencing the art behind it.

Summer in the city is intense, comes with energy from dawn until long after dark. You'll find yourself drawn to rooftop bars where the views are endless, and the atmosphere is buzzing with that unmistakable summer vibe. You should definitely hit up Central Park for SummerStage concerts—outdoor, live, and totally free. Movies in Bryant Park? That's a classic—you bring a blanket, some snacks, and settle in for a film under the stars, surrounded by the city's towering buildings. The Fourth of July fireworks over the East River are something you've got to see—they light up the entire skyline, and finding the perfect spot to watch is an event in itself. If you're into baseball, catch a Yankees game at the stadium—it's not just about the sport, it's about being part of the crowd, the noise, the excitement that you can feel in the air.

Fall is when the city turns gold. The leaves in Central Park and along the Hudson River Greenway create a scene straight out of a postcard. You'll want to take your time, walk slowly, and really soak in the colors—the reds, oranges, and yellows that make the whole city glow. The New York Film Festival is on, and it's your chance to see films that everyone will be talking about later, in venues that make the experience even richer. And Halloween in the city? The

Village Halloween Parade is something you need to see—thousands of people, each more creatively dressed than the last, turning the streets into one massive celebration of the strange and the spectacular. If you're here in late November, the Macy's Thanksgiving Day Parade is a must—it's one of those events that's larger than life, with giant balloons, floats, and the kind of excitement that only happens once a year.

Winter wraps the city in a layer of holiday magic. Rockefeller Center's Christmas tree is iconic, and ice skating there is a must, even if you've never skated before—it's less about skill and more about the experience. You'll find the holiday window displays along Fifth Avenue mesmerizing—each one is a story in itself, told through lights, colors, and creativity. The Bryant Park Winter Village offers holiday shopping, ice skating, and warm drinks to keep the chill away, all in one place that feels cozy despite being in the middle of everything. New Year's Eve in Times Square is chaotic, packed, and unforgettable—if you're up for the crowds, there's nothing like being there when the ball drops, surrounded by the energy of a million people welcoming the new year together. And when it snows, the whole city changes—the parks, the streets, everything takes on a quiet, almost magical quality that you need to see to believe.

Budgeting for Your Trip

Let's get straight to it—planning a trip on a budget doesn't mean sacrificing your experience, and with some careful choices, you can see everything without overspending. First, think about when you're visiting because timing is key. If you avoid the peak times like the holidays or the height of summer, you're going to find flights and accommodations at a much lower cost, and you'll also have the added benefit of enjoying the city without the overwhelming crowds, which means you'll see more, do more, and stress less.

When you're looking for a place to stay, don't feel like you need to be right in the middle of everything. Neighborhoods like Long Island City in Queens or Williamsburg in Brooklyn are perfect—they're close to all the action but much more affordable. These areas are well connected by the subway, so you can get to Manhattan in just a few minutes without paying Manhattan prices, and you'll also discover local cafes, restaurants, and shops that offer great value and a more authentic experience. If you're comfortable with something a little different, consider staying in an Airbnb or a hostel. Airbnb can give you the chance to stay in unique places at a fraction of the cost of a hotel, and hostels offer budget-friendly options with the added bonus of meeting other travelers, which can be part of the fun if you're traveling solo or just want to connect with others during your trip.

Eating well on a budget is easier than you might think, and it's one of the best ways to experience the city. Street food is not just cheap—it's part of the city's culture. Grab a bagel with cream cheese from a local deli for breakfast—it's quick, filling, and gives you a taste of something simple yet iconic. Lunch could be a slice of pizza from Joe's Pizza or a food truck meal, which is affordable, delicious, and fast. For dinner, neighborhoods like Chinatown or the East Village are where you'll find authentic, flavorful meals at prices that won't break the bank—think dim sum, ramen, or a big plate of pasta. Even if you want a more upscale dining experience, look for prix fixe menus, which offer several courses at a set price, often at a significant discount compared to ordering à la carte, so you can enjoy fine dining without the hefty bill.

Seeing the sights without spending a fortune is absolutely possible if you know where to look. Parks like Central Park and the High Line are not just free—they offer some of the best views and experiences in the city, giving you endless places to walk, relax, and take in the scenery without spending a dime. Museums like The Met and MoMA have pay-what-you-wish days or free entry at certain times, which means you can enjoy world-class art and culture on a budget. And if you plan on visiting several paid attractions, investing in a CityPASS is smart—it bundles multiple attractions into one discounted ticket, saving you money while also letting you skip the lines at some of the busiest spots, so you spend more time enjoying and less time waiting.

Getting around the city doesn't have to be expensive, and the subway is your best friend. Buy a MetroCard with an unlimited weekly pass if you're here for a few days—this gives you unlimited rides on subways and buses, and it's way cheaper than using taxis or rideshares for every trip. The subway will get you almost anywhere you want to go quickly and efficiently, and if you're not sure which line to take, just ask someone—it's one of the most affordable and practical ways to see the city. When you do need to use a rideshare, try pooling with others or reserving it for times when you're carrying luggage or heading to the airport—this way, you're not spending more than necessary.

Keep an eye on those small expenses that can add up fast. Carry a reusable water bottle to avoid buying drinks on the go, and use the free Wi-Fi in parks, cafes, and public spaces to stay connected without racking up data charges. If you plan ahead a little, like packing snacks or grabbing a sandwich from a deli to carry with you, you'll avoid those impulse buys that can quickly eat into your budget, allowing you to focus your spending on the experiences that really matter to you, like a special meal or a unique activity.

Choosing the Right Accommodation

When you're deciding where to stay, it's all about matching your accommodation to your needs and budget because the right place can elevate your entire trip, and it's important to find a spot that fits your travel style. If you're looking for luxury, and you want to be right in the middle of everything, consider staying in Midtown, where top hotels like The Plaza or the Mandarin Oriental offer not just comfort but an experience—think stunning views of Central Park, impeccable service, and the convenience of being steps away from Times Square and Broadway. However, these prime locations come with a price, and you'll need to be prepared for the busy atmosphere that comes with staying in such a central area, but if being close to the city's iconic landmarks is your priority, it's worth the investment.

If you're drawn to a more creative, unique atmosphere, and you want to experience the city's trendy side, look at neighborhoods like SoHo or the Lower East Side, where boutique hotels give you a mix of style and comfort. Here, you'll find hotels that aren't just places to sleep but destinations in themselves, with art-filled lobbies, cozy yet chic rooms, and a location that puts you right in the middle of some of the city's best shopping, dining, and nightlife. But remember, while these areas offer a vibrant, exciting experience, the rooms might be smaller, and the prices can be high, so if space and budget are concerns, this might not be your first choice, but the trade-off is being immersed in the city's cultural pulse, where every corner has something to discover.

For a more budget-friendly stay that doesn't sacrifice location or experience, consider Long Island City in Queens or Williamsburg in Brooklyn, where you can find modern, affordable hotels that offer great views and easy access to the city. These neighborhoods are a smart choice if you want to save money while still being close to Manhattan, with the added bonus of exploring areas that are rich with local character, offering a different perspective on the city, with unique shops, cafes, and a more laid-back vibe. The subway will get you to the heart of the city quickly, so you're not far from the action, but you'll have the benefit of staying in a quieter, less crowded area, which can make your trip more relaxed and enjoyable.

If you're staying longer or want a more home-like experience, an Airbnb might be your best option, especially in neighborhoods like Harlem, the East Village, or Greenpoint, where you can find a variety of spaces that suit your needs. Airbnb gives you the flexibility to have more space, a kitchen for preparing meals, and a chance to live more like a local, but keep in mind, you won't have the same services as a hotel, like daily housekeeping or a concierge, so it's ideal if you prefer a bit more independence during your stay and enjoy immersing yourself in the local community.

The key is to think about what you value most in your accommodation—is it the convenience of being close to major attractions, the vibe of staying in a trendy, artistic area, the cost savings of being in a less central neighborhood, or the comfort of having a home away from home? By focusing on what matters most to you, you can choose a place that enhances your experience and makes your trip everything you want it to be, ensuring that you're comfortable, connected, and ready to explore all that the city has to offer.

Packing Essentials: What to Bring

You need to pack smart for this trip, and the key is bringing the right essentials that prepare you for everything the city throws your way, from unpredictable weather to endless walking. Start with layers because the weather can shift quickly, and having a lightweight, waterproof jacket is a must to keep you dry without weighing you down. Bring a couple of versatile sweaters or hoodies that you can layer over t-shirts or under a jacket, making sure you're ready for anything from cool mornings to warmer afternoons, all while staying comfortable and prepared.

Your footwear is crucial, so pack shoes that you can walk in all day long. You'll be covering a lot of ground, so think about well-cushioned, supportive shoes like broken-in sneakers or comfortable flats that you know won't give you blisters. If you're visiting in winter, don't forget waterproof boots to keep your feet warm and dry because cold, wet feet can ruin your day faster than anything else, and you'll be spending a lot of time outdoors.

A portable phone charger is something you absolutely need because your phone will be your lifeline for navigation, photos, and keeping in touch, and a dead battery means being disconnected at the worst possible moment, so make sure you have a charger that's reliable and easy to carry. Keep everything secure with a small crossbody bag or a backpack that's easy to carry and keeps your essentials safe, especially in busy areas where you'll want to keep your belongings close and your hands free for taking pictures or grabbing a quick snack.

Stay hydrated by packing a reusable water bottle because it's easy to forget to drink enough when you're on the move, but having a bottle with you means you can fill up whenever you need to, saving money and staying refreshed. If you're visiting in summer, protect yourself from the sun by packing sunscreen, sunglasses, and a hat because the last thing you want is to end up sunburned and uncomfortable when you've still got hours of exploring ahead. For winter trips, make sure you've got a warm coat, gloves, a scarf, and a hat, because the cold can be intense, and staying warm is key to enjoying your time outdoors without cutting it short because you're freezing.

Pack for your plans, too. If you've got a nice dinner or a show on your itinerary, bring one dressier outfit that can easily transition from day to night, and if you're planning on spending your days walking around parks or visiting casual spots, stick to comfortable, casual clothes that keep you relaxed and ready for anything. A small, foldable tote bag is also handy for carrying anything extra you pick up along the way because it saves you from juggling too many bags and can be tucked away when you don't need it.

Your packing list should be about essentials that keep you comfortable, prepared, and ready to enjoy your trip without any unnecessary stress. Stick to what you know you'll need, focus on comfort and versatility, and make sure everything you bring is something that will enhance your experience, not weigh you down or take up space unnecessarily. By packing smart, you'll be able to fully enjoy every moment, knowing you've got everything you need to handle whatever the city has in store for you.

Travel Insurance and Safety Tips

You need travel insurance because it protects you from unexpected problems that can ruin your trip and cost you a lot of money, like if you get sick and need medical help, or if your luggage gets lost and you're left without your things, or if you have to cancel your trip at the last minute. Make sure your insurance covers medical emergencies, trip cancellations, and lost or delayed baggage because these are the most important areas that can cause serious headaches if something goes wrong. Having insurance means you're not on your own when things don't go as planned, and it can save you from facing huge bills or stressful situations without support.

When you're in the city, stay aware of your surroundings because crowded places are where you need to be extra careful with your belongings. Keep your things close and secure, like using a crossbody bag that zips up or a money belt that stays hidden because this makes it much harder for pickpockets to target you, especially in busy areas like subway stations or popular tourist spots. If you're using your phone in public, don't get too absorbed—keep one eye on what's happening around you because it's easy to miss someone getting too close when you're focused on your screen. If something feels off, trust your instincts and move to a safer area or ask for help.

Being prepared makes all the difference, so know how you'll get around, have emergency numbers handy, and keep someone back home informed of your plans, because it's all about having a plan and staying connected so you're not caught off guard. Use apps to navigate safely and stick to well-lit, populated routes at night, because these small steps keep you in control of your experience and let you enjoy your trip without unnecessary worries. With travel insurance and a bit of street smarts, you can focus on enjoying everything the city has to offer, knowing you're covered and ready for anything that might come your way.

CHAPTER 3
NAVIGATING THE BIG APPLE

Getting to New York: Airports and Transfers

Getting from the airport to your destination is your first step, and knowing the best way to do that can make your arrival much smoother, so let's break it down clearly.

If you're flying into JFK, which is about 15 miles from Midtown Manhattan, the most straightforward and cost-effective option is to take the AirTrain to Jamaica Station and then hop on the subway. This route is reliable and affordable, but you should expect it to take around an hour or more, depending on where exactly you're heading. If you're not up for navigating public transport with your luggage, taking a taxi is the easiest choice—taxis from JFK have a flat rate to Manhattan, giving you a predictable fare and a direct ride to your hotel in about 45 minutes to an hour, depending on traffic.

At LaGuardia, which is closer at just 8 miles from Midtown, you won't find a subway connection, so you'll need to decide between the bus or a taxi. The Q70 LaGuardia Link bus connects you to the subway at Jackson Heights or Roosevelt Avenue, making it a budget-friendly option, but it can be crowded, especially during peak times, so if you prefer a quicker, more comfortable ride, grabbing a taxi is your best bet. In this case, you're looking at around 30 to 45 minutes to reach the city, depending on traffic, and it's the simplest way to avoid the hassle of public transport, especially if you've got luggage.

If you're arriving at Newark, which is across the Hudson River in New Jersey, about 16 miles from Midtown Manhattan, the AirTrain Newark to NJ Transit is the fastest and most cost-effective option, getting you to Penn Station in about 30 minutes once you're on the train. For those who prefer a direct ride, a taxi or ride-share will take you directly to your destination, although it will be more expensive due to the distance and crossing into New York City. This option is worth considering if you want to avoid any delays and head straight to your hotel without the hassle of managing bags on public transport.

Whatever your choice, plan ahead to make sure your transfer is smooth because dealing with this as soon as you land makes your arrival easier and sets the right tone for your trip. Booking a car service in advance is an option that many find convenient, letting you skip the wait and head directly to your destination without any extra stress, so think about what will make your arrival easiest and most comfortable for you.

Public Transportation Guide

Navigating the city's public transportation system is all about making your life easier and moving through the city quickly and efficiently. You're going to rely heavily on the subway because it's the fastest way to get around, and once you understand how it works, you'll see why everyone uses it. Get yourself a MetroCard as soon as you arrive—it's your key to the subway and buses. Load it with enough credit to last a few days so you're not constantly refilling. Swipe your MetroCard at the turnstile, step through, and follow the signs—just make sure you're on the right platform, heading in the right direction, whether it's uptown or downtown because getting on the wrong train can send you far from where you want to be. Check the signs and listen for the announcements so you know exactly where to get off—each stop is clearly marked, but it's better to stay alert than miss your stop, especially if you need to transfer to another line.

If you're traveling during rush hours, you'll want to avoid the busiest times, like early morning or late afternoon, because the subway can get packed, and it's not always the most comfortable ride, so try to travel just before or after these peaks to have a little more breathing room. When you're on the train, move away from the doors to let others on and off easily—it's a simple way to keep the flow going and avoid the crush of people trying to get on or off at busy stations.

Buses are another option, particularly if you need to travel above ground or if you're heading to areas that aren't well served by the subway. You'll use your MetroCard here too—just dip it into the reader when you board. Buses are slower than the subway, especially in heavy traffic, so they're best for shorter trips or if you're not in a rush, but they do give you a view of the city as you go, which can be a nice change of pace from the underground. Pay attention to the route and the upcoming stops so you know when to get off—it's announced, but it's easy to get distracted, so stay aware.

Sometimes, though, you'll need a quicker, more direct option, and that's where taxis come in handy. Hailing a taxi is easy—just step to the curb and raise your hand when you see one with the roof light on, indicating it's available. Once inside, tell the driver where you're headed, sit back, and watch the meter—taxis are metered, so you'll know exactly how much you're paying, and when you arrive, you can settle up by cash or card. Remember to tip your driver, around 15-20%, because it's customary and ensures good service.

To make sure you're always on the best route, use transit apps like Citymapper or Google Maps, which give you real-time updates and help you avoid service changes or delays. Always keep your belongings close and be aware of your surroundings, especially in crowded stations or on packed trains and buses, because staying alert helps you move through the city smoothly and safely. With a little practice, you'll find that getting around is straightforward, and soon enough, you'll be navigating the city's transit system like a pro, with confidence and ease.

Walking and Biking Tips

Walking and biking are the best ways to truly see the city because they let you connect with your surroundings in a way that no other mode of transport can, and if you plan it right, you can make the most of your time while staying safe and enjoying every moment. When you're walking, focus on routes that give you a mix of the city's energy and its quieter, scenic spots. The **High Line** is a perfect

example—it's an elevated park that runs through the city's west side, offering incredible views of the Hudson River and the surrounding neighborhoods, and it's a spot where you can walk without worrying about traffic, surrounded by gardens, art, and some of the best views you'll find in the city. Start at the Gansevoort Street entrance and make your way north to Hudson Yards, where you can take your time, stop to rest on one of the benches, and just soak in the atmosphere because this is a walk that's all about enjoying the journey as much as the destination.

Central Park is another must-do for walking because it's not just a park—it's a world of its own, with winding paths that take you through different landscapes, from the open, sun-drenched fields of Sheep Meadow to the tranquil, tree-shaded paths of The Ramble, where it's easy to forget you're in the middle of one of the busiest cities in the world. Head towards Bethesda Terrace if you want to see one of the park's most iconic spots, where the fountain and the lake make for a perfect place to pause and take in the view, or walk along The Mall, where the canopy of trees creates a beautiful, almost cinematic experience, especially in the early morning or late afternoon when the light is softest.

If you're biking, the Hudson River Greenway is your go-to route because it's safe, scenic, and stretches along the west side of the city from Battery Park up to the George Washington Bridge, offering uninterrupted views of the river and the skyline. Start your ride early in the morning when the path is quieter, and you'll find it's not just a way to get from point A to point B but an experience in itself, with places to stop and enjoy the view, whether you're looking out at the water or back at the city's iconic buildings. Central Park also offers some of the best biking in the city, with loops that take you through the entire park, letting you see everything from the manicured lawns to the more rugged, wooded areas. Start your ride at the southern end near Columbus Circle and follow the loop all the way up to the northern tip at Harlem Meer, where you can take in the full diversity of the park's landscapes.

Safety is key whether you're walking or biking, so always stay alert, especially at intersections and busy areas where cars, bikes, and pedestrians all share the space, and remember that the best way to enjoy your walk or ride is to do it at a time when the city is a bit calmer, like early in the morning or later in the afternoon, when the light is beautiful and the streets and paths are less crowded. If you're biking, always wear a helmet, stick to bike lanes, and be aware of your surroundings—watch for car doors opening or pedestrians stepping into the bike lanes, and always be ready to stop if something unexpected happens. Walking and biking give you a unique perspective on the city, letting you see it at your own pace, discover hidden gems, and experience the everyday life of the city in a way that's both immersive and personal, so take your time, stay safe, and enjoy every moment.

Maps and Navigation Tools

To get around the city smoothly, you need to know how to use both digital maps and paper maps because they each have their strengths, and combining them will make your navigation easier and stress-free. Start with Google Maps or Citymapper, which are your best tools for moving quickly from one place to another. With Google Maps, you type in where you want to go, pick your mode of transport—whether you're walking, biking, or using the subway—and it gives you exact directions that update as you move, so you always know where you're going. Citymapper is even more detailed when it comes to public transportation, showing you the best subway or bus routes and giving you real-time updates on any delays, so you never waste time standing around or taking the wrong train. These apps are straightforward and help you plan your day with confidence, letting you save important locations like your hotel or favorite spots so that you can pull them up quickly when you need directions.

But don't rely only on your phone because a paper map is incredibly useful, especially when you want to see the bigger picture of where you are and where you're going. You can grab a free map from your hotel or a visitor center, and it's a great way to get a sense of the area without needing to constantly check your phone. A paper map gives you an overview that helps you understand the layout of neighborhoods, showing you how streets connect and where landmarks are in relation to each other. This makes it easier to plan a walking route through a neighborhood or a day in the park, giving you a clear idea of your surroundings. Plus, paper maps don't run out of battery or lose signal, so they're a reliable backup if your phone dies or you find yourself in an area with spotty reception, ensuring you're never completely lost.

Using both digital and paper maps together is the smartest way to navigate because it gives you flexibility. For instance, you can use Google Maps to get walking directions to a museum, then switch to a paper map to explore the area around it, which helps you find interesting spots you might otherwise miss. If you're in Central Park, a paper map lets you see all the trails and landmarks at once, helping you decide which areas to explore, and once you're done, Google Maps can guide you to your next stop quickly, making sure you stay on track.

Navigating the city doesn't have to be stressful because with the right tools, you're always in control of where you're going. Whether you're navigating busy streets or planning a relaxed day of exploration, using both types of maps will make your experience much smoother and more enjoyable, giving you the confidence to explore everything the city has to offer without any worries.

Understanding New York Etiquette

When you're here, understanding the social norms will make your experience smoother and help you fit in right away. On the subway, things move fast, so make sure you stand clear of the doors and let people exit before you step on because pushing your way in is not just rude—it slows everyone down, and time matters here. Once you're on, if you're carrying a bag, keep it on your lap or at your feet because space is tight, and during busy hours, move to the center of the car to make room for others because blocking the door isn't just annoying, it's a sure way to irritate everyone around you. If you're sitting, be ready to give up your seat if someone older, pregnant, or with a disability gets on because showing that kind of respect isn't just appreciated—it's expected. And remember, subway cars are quiet spaces—people don't talk much, so keep any conversations short and low, and if you're listening to music, make sure nobody else can hear it because people value their peace in these packed spaces.

When it comes to eating out, tipping is essential because it's how servers make their living, so you need to tip about 20% of your bill because that's the standard, and leaving less is just not okay. If the place is busy, be mindful of how long you stay because others are waiting for tables, and holding things up isn't considerate, especially when the restaurant is turning tables quickly. At counter-service spots, dropping a dollar or two in the tip jar is a good move, especially if the service is solid or they go out of their way to make your visit better because every little bit helps and shows you appreciate their effort.

In public spaces, personal space is crucial because it's crowded here, and people need their space respected to keep things moving smoothly. When you're walking, stay to the right and keep a steady pace because people walk with purpose, and if you suddenly stop or block the way, you're going to frustrate those who are in a hurry, so if you need to check your phone or pause, step aside to do it. And don't worry if someone bumps into you—keep moving because it's not personal, just the reality of a busy city, and stopping to react will only slow you down and add unnecessary stress.

To blend in, you need to pick up on these cues and move with the city's rhythm because doing so makes everything easier and lets you enjoy your time without any unnecessary tension. Being aware of these simple rules means you're more likely to have a positive experience, and you'll find it easier to navigate everything the city has to offer, fitting right into the daily flow and making the most of your visit.

CHAPTER 4
DISCOVERING THE NEIGHBORHOODS

Manhattan: The Heart of the City

Manhattan is the core of the city, and each neighborhood offers a distinct experience that captures the essence of this vibrant place, so if you're looking for the most intense energy, head straight to Times Square, where the streets are always packed, and the lights are brighter than anything you've ever seen. Here, everything is larger than life, from the towering billboards to the bustling crowds that seem to move in every direction at once because this is the entertainment hub, where Broadway shows draw in visitors from around the world, and the constant buzz of activity never stops, making it a place where you can feel the city's pulse at any hour of the day or night.

But just a short walk from the chaos of Times Square, you'll find a completely different vibe in Central Park, which is like stepping into another world where the city's noise fades away, and you're surrounded by greenery and open space, so take your time exploring its many paths and hidden spots because this isn't just a park—it's a massive, sprawling escape right in the middle of everything, offering you a chance to breathe and unwind. Whether you're rowing a boat on the lake, lounging on the Great Lawn, or wandering through The Ramble, each part of the park offers a unique experience, so spend a few hours here to recharge before diving back into the city's fast pace.

If you want to experience the city's charm and history, head to Greenwich

Village, where the atmosphere slows down, and the streets are lined with trees, historic brownstones, and small, independent shops that give the neighborhood its unique character because this is where you'll find cozy cafes, hidden jazz clubs, and off-Broadway theaters that capture the creative spirit of the city. Washington Square Park is the heart of the Village, where the iconic arch frames a lively scene of street performers, students, and locals, making it the perfect spot to sit and soak in the vibe of the neighborhood, so take a stroll through the narrow streets of the West Village, where each turn reveals something new, from quaint bookstores to some of the best restaurants in the city.

For a deeper dive into the city's history, explore the Financial District, where you'll walk among towering skyscrapers that tell the story of the city's rise as a global financial power, so don't miss Wall Street, where the New York Stock Exchange is the focal point of the world's markets, and take a moment to visit Trinity Church, one of the oldest buildings in the city, which stands as a reminder of the city's long history. From here, make your way to Battery Park, where you can catch views of the Statue of Liberty and Ellis Island, both symbols of the city's role as a gateway to America, and spend some time at the 9/11 Memorial, where the city's resilience is honored, offering a powerful and emotional experience that's a must-see for any visitor.

Up in Harlem, the energy shifts again, offering you a rich cultural experience that's deeply rooted in the city's African American heritage, so take a walk along 125th Street, where you'll find the legendary Apollo Theater, a cornerstone of the neighborhood's vibrant music scene, and explore the local restaurants that serve up some of the best soul food you'll ever taste. Harlem is where history and culture come together, creating a neighborhood that's as dynamic as it is welcoming, so take your time here, whether you're catching a live jazz performance or simply walking through the neighborhood to get a feel for its unique character.

Each of these neighborhoods offers something different, from the high energy of Times Square to the peaceful paths of Central Park, the historic charm of Greenwich Village, the powerful history of the Financial District, and the cultural richness of Harlem, so make sure you explore them all to get a full sense of what Manhattan is really about. By diving into the unique vibes of each area, you'll experience the diversity that makes this place so special, and you'll leave with a true understanding of why Manhattan is the beating heart of the city, filled with endless possibilities and unforgettable experiences.

Brooklyn: Hipster Havens and Historic Streets

Brooklyn is where creativity and history come together, so if you want to experience the best of it, start with Williamsburg because this neighborhood is the center of Brooklyn's hip culture. You'll find streets full of art galleries, boutique shops, and cafes that make some of the best coffee in the city because Williamsburg is known for its vibrant street art and converted warehouses, which now house everything from vintage stores to rooftop bars with stunning views of the skyline, and it's the perfect place to explore if you're looking for that mix of old industrial charm and cutting-edge style. Walk along Bedford Avenue because that's where the action is, and don't miss Smorgasburg, an open-air food market where you can try all kinds of amazing food, from artisanal treats to global flavors, and it's a great spot to grab something delicious and enjoy the lively atmosphere.

Just a quick trip away, you'll find Brooklyn Heights, a neighborhood that couldn't be more different from Williamsburg but is just as captivating because here, the streets are quieter, lined with beautiful 19th-century brownstones, and the vibe is more about classic charm and stunning views. Take a walk along the Promenade because this walkway offers one of the best views of the Manhattan skyline, the Brooklyn Bridge, and the Statue of Liberty because it's a place where you can take in the beauty of the city in a more relaxed, peaceful setting, away from the hustle and bustle. The historic homes and calm, tree-lined streets of Brooklyn Heights make it the perfect place for a leisurely stroll, and it's easy to lose yourself in the charm of this neighborhood, where each turn reveals another picture-perfect scene.

Bushwick is where you go to see Brooklyn's most vibrant and raw creativity because this neighborhood is all about street art and the edgy, artistic energy that makes Brooklyn so unique. The walls of Bushwick are covered in some of the most impressive murals you'll find anywhere, and they change regularly, so there's always something new to see because the Bushwick Collective is a must-visit for anyone who loves art, and walking through the streets here feels like exploring an open-air gallery. But Bushwick isn't just about what's on the walls because the neighborhood is also home to some of the city's most interesting galleries and performance spaces, where you can catch everything from live music to experimental theater in spaces that are as creative as the work they showcase.

When it comes to food, Brooklyn delivers, whether you're after a classic New York slice or something more adventurous because in Williamsburg, Roberta's is the place to go for wood-fired pizza that's worth the hype, and Peter Luger Steak House in South Williamsburg is legendary for a reason—it's where you go for a steak that's as iconic as the city itself. In Brooklyn Heights, The River Café offers not just a meal but an experience, with its stunning views of Manhattan making every bite more memorable, so make sure to explore the local bakeries and coffee shops too, where the pastries are as rich in history as the neighborhood.

Brooklyn is full of surprises, and it's in the small, unexpected places that you'll find its true spirit because neighborhoods like Greenpoint and DUMBO offer their own unique blend of old and new. In Greenpoint, you'll discover traditional Polish bakeries sitting alongside some of the trendiest bars in the city, making it a neighborhood that's as diverse as it is charming, and in DUMBO, the cobblestone streets and waterfront views create a stunning backdrop for exploring the area's galleries, shops, and restaurants, where you can enjoy everything from artisanal goods to contemporary art.

Each part of Brooklyn has its own character, from the trendsetting streets of Williamsburg to the historic beauty of Brooklyn Heights and the artistic pulse of Bushwick because exploring these neighborhoods will give you a true sense of what makes Brooklyn such an essential part of the city's identity. Take your time to delve into what each area has to offer because by the end of your journey, you'll have experienced a side of the city that's as diverse and dynamic as the people who live here, and that's something you won't forget.

Queens: A Global Melting Pot

Queens is where the world meets in one borough, and each neighborhood gives you a chance to dive deep into different cultures, so start with Flushing, a neighborhood that's a hub of Asian culture and home to one of the most authentic Chinatowns in the city, filled with bustling markets and some of the best food you'll find anywhere. Walk down Main Street, where you'll see a mix of shops, food stalls, and restaurants that offer everything from fresh dumplings to exotic spices because this is the place to go if you want to taste and experience East Asia without leaving the city. Make sure to visit Nan Xiang Xiao Long Bao because their soup dumplings are legendary, packed with rich broth and tender meat that make them a must-try, and while you're in the area, take a break at the Queens Botanical Garden, a peaceful spot where you can enjoy beautifully curated landscapes that reflect the cultural diversity of the neighborhood.

Next, head over to Astoria, where the Greek influence is strong, and the streets are filled with traditional bakeries, tavernas, and markets that make you feel like you've stepped into a Mediterranean village because this neighborhood has been the heart of the Greek community for generations. Start with a meal at Taverna Kyclades because they serve some of the freshest seafood you'll find, grilled to perfection and paired with classic sides like lemon potatoes that are full of flavor, and as you explore, you'll notice the mix of old and new, with historic Greek shops sitting alongside modern cafes and boutiques that keep the area vibrant and evolving. Don't forget to check out the Museum of the Moving Image because it's a fascinating dive into the history of film and television, offering a cultural experience that's a perfect complement to your day in Astoria, and if you're looking to relax, head to Astoria Park, where you can enjoy stunning views of the East River and the Manhattan skyline while taking in the local atmosphere.

Jackson Heights is where you'll find the city's South Asian community at its most vibrant, with streets filled with the colors, sounds, and smells of India, Pakistan, and Bangladesh, so make sure to walk along 74th Street, known as "Little India," because this is where you'll find shops selling vibrant saris, intricate jewelry, and spices that will make your mouth water. Stop by Jackson Diner because it's famous for its buffet that offers a wide range of dishes, from rich curries to freshly baked naan, making it the perfect place to sample the best of Indian cuisine, and don't miss the sweet shops in the area because they offer traditional desserts like gulab jamun that are a must-try, or grab a few samosas to snack on as you explore the lively streets.

Corona is where you go to experience the heart of the city's Latin American community because the energy here is high, and the food and music reflect the vibrant cultures of Mexico, the Dominican Republic, and beyond. Head to Tortilleria Nixtamal because they make their tortillas fresh every day, and the tacos are packed with flavor, offering a taste of Mexico that's as authentic as it gets, and while you're in the neighborhood, visit the Louis Armstrong House Museum because it gives you a glimpse into the life of the jazz legend, offering a unique cultural experience that connects you to the history and spirit of the area.

Queens offers a unique chance to experience the world without leaving the city, and each neighborhood is a gateway to a different culture, so take your time to explore the vibrant streets, taste the authentic food, and immerse yourself in the diverse communities that make this borough so special because by the end of your journey, you'll have experienced the true essence of what makes Queens a global melting pot, and those memories will stay with you long after you've left.

The Bronx: Culture and Green Spaces

The Bronx offers you a mix of culture and nature that's hard to find anywhere else in the city, so let's focus on what makes this borough a must-visit, starting with the Bronx Zoo, which is one of the largest and most renowned zoos in the world, where you'll find yourself surrounded by wildlife from every corner of the globe, from the majestic lions in the African Plains to the playful sea lions that always draw a crowd. It's not just about seeing animals—it's about experiencing a place dedicated to conservation and education, where every exhibit teaches you something new, and if you're here, make sure you take the monorail ride because it gives you a different perspective on the zoo's vast, naturalistic habitats, making it more than just a visit but a journey through the world's ecosystems.

Right next door is the New York Botanical Garden, an oasis where you can wander through 250 acres of stunning gardens, each one showcasing the beauty of plant life from around the world, so start with the Rose Garden if you're visiting in the summer because it's a spectacular display of color and fragrance that's hard to forget, and if you prefer something more tropical, the Enid A. Haupt Conservatory is where you'll find lush, vibrant plants that transport you to a completely different climate, offering a perfect escape from the city's rush. Every season brings a new experience here, so if you're around in the winter, don't miss the holiday train show because it's a magical exhibit that transforms the garden into a miniature city, making it a highlight of the winter season, and no matter when you visit, the Botanical Garden offers a peaceful retreat where you can connect with nature in a way that's both relaxing and inspiring.

If you're into sports, Yankee Stadium is where you need to be because this is more than just a baseball field—it's a shrine to one of the most successful teams in sports history, and when you walk through the gates, you feel the energy and tradition that come with being in the home of the New York Yankees. If you have time, take a tour to see Monument Park, where the greatest Yankees are honored, and visit the Yankees Museum, filled with memorabilia that tells the story of the team's legendary past, but if you can catch a game, do it because there's nothing like being in the stadium, surrounded by passionate fans, cheering for one of the most iconic teams in the world, and it's an experience that connects you directly to the spirit of the Bronx.

The Bronx is also a place where culture thrives, with a strong community vibe that drives the local art scene, so check out the Bronx Museum of the Arts, where you'll find contemporary works that reflect the borough's diverse cultural landscape, offering perspectives that are as dynamic as the community itself, and if you're interested in photography and documentary work, the Bronx Documentary Center is a must because it features powerful exhibits that focus on social issues and community stories, giving you a deeper understanding of the borough's vibrant and resilient spirit.

For those who love the outdoors, the green spaces in The Bronx are some of the best in the city, and Pelham Bay Park is the perfect example of that because it's the largest park in the city, offering miles of trails, a beautiful coastline, and the historic Bartow-Pell Mansion, where you can explore the elegant estate and its gardens, which are a window into the area's past, and if you're looking for something closer to the center of the borough, Van Cortlandt Park is a great option because it's got everything from hiking trails to a historic house museum that dates back to the 18th century, giving you a mix of nature and history in one place. These parks aren't just for relaxing—they're where the community comes together for festivals, sports, and cultural events, making them a central part of life in the Bronx, and spending time here gives you a true sense of the borough's character, blending natural beauty with a deep sense of history and community.

The Bronx is all about that perfect blend of culture, history, and natural beauty, offering you experiences that are as diverse as the borough itself, so whether you're exploring the Bronx Zoo, relaxing in the Botanical Garden, cheering on the Yankees, or immersing yourself in the local art scene, you're connecting with the heart of the Bronx, a place that's rich in tradition and full of life, and by the time you leave, you'll have a deeper appreciation for what makes this borough so unique, with memories that capture the essence of its culture and the warmth of its community.

Staten Island: A Quiet Escape

Staten Island is where you go to escape the city's noise and find a peaceful retreat, starting with the Staten Island Ferry, which gives you the most stunning views of the Statue of Liberty and the Manhattan skyline, all for free, and this ferry ride is the perfect way to slow down and enjoy the beauty of the harbor as you make your way to the island. Once you arrive, head straight to Historic Richmond Town because this living history village is where you can walk through centuries-old streets and feel like you've stepped back in time, with well-preserved buildings that show you exactly how life was during the colonial era, so take your time exploring the old houses, the general store, and the working farm, where you'll see traditional crafts being practiced just as they were hundreds of years ago, giving you a deep connection to the past in a way that's both real and tangible.

For a dose of nature, the Staten Island Greenbelt is your go-to, with over 2,800 acres of parks and forests that make it feel like you've truly escaped the city, and within the Greenbelt, High Rock Park is a standout because its quiet trails wind through dense woods and around serene ponds, offering a peaceful retreat where you can hike, explore, and just breathe in the fresh air, far from the city's hustle, and if you're interested in gardens, the Staten Island Botanical Garden at Snug Harbor is a must-see, with its beautiful array of gardens, including the tranquil Chinese Scholar's Garden, where you can stroll through bamboo groves and intricate rockeries, and the vibrant rose gardens, each offering a unique space to relax and enjoy the natural beauty.

Don't miss Conference House Park at the southern tip of the island because it's a place where history meets nature, with the historic Conference House, a 17th-century mansion that played a key role in American history, surrounded by beautiful grounds with expansive views of the Raritan Bay, and here, you can walk along the waterfront, explore the historic house, and find a sense of peace that's a world away from the busy city, making it the perfect spot for a quiet escape.

Staten Island is all about slowing down and taking in the simple joys, whether you're exploring the rich history of Richmond Town, hiking through the Greenbelt's peaceful trails, or just enjoying the scenic ferry ride that brings you here, so if you're looking for a break from the fast pace of the city, this is where you'll find the calm and quiet you need, in a place where nature and history combine to offer a truly relaxing experience.

CHAPTER 5
ICONIC AND HIDDEN ATTRACTIONS

Iconic Landmarks

The city's most iconic landmarks are essential stops on your visit because they capture the spirit and history of this incredible place, starting with the Statue of Liberty, which is not just a statue—it's a powerful symbol of freedom and hope that has stood tall in the harbor for over a century, so when you visit, take the first ferry from Battery Park early in the morning to avoid the crowds because this gives you the best chance to explore Liberty Island without feeling rushed, and if you want a truly unforgettable experience, make sure you book your tickets in advance to climb up to the crown where the view over the harbor is absolutely stunning, offering a perspective that's as inspiring as the statue itself.

Then, you'll want to visit the Empire State Building, an iconic piece of the city's skyline that has been a symbol of ambition and innovation since 1931, and when you stand on the 86th-floor observation deck, you'll see the entire city spread out below you because this view is like no other, giving you a true sense of the city's vastness and energy, so to avoid the biggest crowds, plan your visit early in the morning or later in the evening when the lines are shorter, letting you take your time and really enjoy the moment, and be sure to check out the building at night because the lights change to mark special occasions, turning it into a colorful beacon that reflects the city's dynamic nature.

Next, you can't miss Times Square, the place where the city's energy is most intense, with its enormous digital billboards and the constant flow of people from all around the world, so for the best experience, visit at night when the lights are brightest, creating an atmosphere that's electric and completely unique to this part of the city. Walking through Times Square, you'll feel like you're at the center of it all, and if you're interested in catching a Broadway show, this is where you'll find the most famous theaters, offering performances that are world-renowned, and for a quieter moment, consider visiting early in the morning when the area is less crowded, giving you a chance to take in the sights without the usual rush of people, making it easier to appreciate the scale and spectacle of the place.

These landmarks aren't just popular tourist spots—they're deeply woven into the fabric of the city, offering you a connection to its history, culture, and unmatched energy, so when you visit, make sure you plan your timing carefully to avoid the busiest times, and give yourself the space to really take in what these sites represent because these experiences will be some of the most memorable of your entire visit, giving you a true sense of what makes the city so iconic.

World-Class Museums

When you're exploring the city's world-class museums, you absolutely have to start with The Met because this isn't just a museum—it's a journey through art and history that spans thousands of years, so when you go, focus on key sections to make the most of your visit. Head straight to the Egyptian Wing, where you can see the Temple of Dendur, an ancient temple that's been perfectly reconstructed inside the museum, surrounded by water, which gives it an almost magical quality that transports you back to ancient times, and then make sure you visit the European Paintings section, where you'll find masterpieces by artists like Rembrandt, Vermeer, and Van Gogh because these works are some of the most famous in the world, and seeing them in person is an experience that stays with you, so if you're short on time, grab a map and focus on these highlights because they're truly the heart of The Met.

Next, head to MoMA, the place for modern and contemporary art, and start on the fifth floor where the museum's most famous pieces are displayed, including Van Gogh's "Starry Night," which is even more impressive when you're standing in front of it, with its swirling blues and vibrant yellows pulling you in, so from there, move on to Picasso's "Les Demoiselles d'Avignon," a painting that's revolutionary in its bold, fragmented depiction of the female form, and you can't miss Salvador Dalí's "The Persistence of Memory," where the melting clocks have become a symbol of surrealism. To get the most out of MoMA, visit on a weekday morning when it's less crowded because this allows you to really appreciate these masterpieces up close without the rush of the crowds.

The American Museum of Natural History is a completely different experience, filled with wonders of the natural world, and you should start with the Hall of Saurischian Dinosaurs, where the massive T. rex skeleton will leave you in awe of its sheer size and power, making it one of the museum's most popular exhibits, and from there, head to the Hall of Ocean Life, where you'll be greeted by a 94-foot-long model of a blue whale suspended from the ceiling, a sight that really puts the scale of these incredible creatures into perspective. If you're into space, the Rose Center for Earth and Space is where you need to be, especially the Hayden Planetarium, which offers a breathtaking journey through the universe, and to make the most of your time, arrive early because this museum can get very crowded, and focus on the dinosaur exhibits, the ocean life hall, and the planetarium to ensure you see the highlights.

These museums are not just places to visit—they are experiences that deepen your understanding of art, history, and science, so plan your visits carefully to avoid the busiest times, focus on the must-see exhibits, and use any resources available, like maps or tours, to navigate these vast collections efficiently because with just a bit of planning, you'll come away with a richer, more meaningful experience that you'll carry with you long after you've left.

Hidden Gems and Local Favorites

To truly experience the city beyond the usual sights, you need to explore its hidden gems, the places that most tourists miss but locals cherish, so start with the Elizabeth Street Garden in Nolita because this small community garden is a peaceful escape, tucked away between buildings, where you can relax among sculptures and greenery, offering a quiet retreat from the city's noise, and it's the kind of spot where you can sit and read or just enjoy a moment of calm in the heart of the city.

For something different in the nightlife scene, you should seek out speakeasies like PDT (Please Don't Tell) in the East Village, a hidden bar that you enter through a vintage phone booth inside Crif Dogs, and this isn't just a bar—it's an experience, with expertly crafted cocktails served in a cozy, intimate setting that feels like a step back in time, so be sure to make a reservation because this place fills up quickly, and the atmosphere is unlike any other, making it a must-visit if you're looking for a unique night out.

When it comes to museums, skip the big crowds and head to the Museum of the Moving Image in Astoria, Queens, where you'll find a deep dive into the history and technology of film, television, and digital media, and this museum is a hidden treasure for film buffs, with exhibits that let you explore everything from classic movie posters to interactive experiences where you can try your hand at film editing or voice acting, giving you a behind-the-scenes look at the magic of movies and TV. It's less crowded than the more famous museums, which means you can take your time and really appreciate what's on display, so if you're passionate about film or just curious about how your favorite shows are made, this is the place to go.

For a peaceful walk that offers a glimpse into the city's history, visit Green-Wood Cemetery in Brooklyn, where you'll find winding paths, rolling hills, and some of the most beautiful views of the skyline from certain points, and this historic cemetery is not just a final resting place for many famous figures—it's a serene park that feels like a hidden sanctuary, especially in the fall when the leaves change color, creating a breathtaking backdrop that's perfect for reflection and relaxation.

If you're into shopping, Artists & Fleas in Williamsburg is the spot to find unique, handcrafted items, from vintage clothing to local art, and this market is filled with independent vendors who bring a creative energy that makes every visit feel like a treasure hunt, so whether you're looking for a special souvenir or just want to browse through one-of-a-kind items, this is where you'll find something truly original, and it's a favorite among locals who appreciate the art and craftsmanship on display.

These hidden gems and local favorites offer you a chance to see the city from a different perspective, one that's more authentic and less crowded, so take the time to explore these spots, ask locals for their recommendations, and venture off the beaten path because that's where you'll discover the real essence of the city, the places that make it special and memorable, giving you experiences that are truly unique to your visit.

CHAPTER 6
DIVE INTO NEW YORK'S CULTURE

New York's Diverse Food Scene

The city's food scene is a must-experience, reflecting the incredible diversity of its neighborhoods, so when you're here, you need to dive into the flavors that make this place one of the best culinary destinations in the world, starting with the street food, which is where you'll find some of the most authentic tastes. You can't leave without trying a classic hot dog, but if you really want to taste something unforgettable, go to a Halal cart, especially around 53rd Street and 6th Avenue, where you'll find gyros packed with tender chicken or lamb, drizzled with white sauce and hot sauce, a combination that's full of flavor and a perfect way to fuel up as you explore.

For a slice of the city's best pizza, head to Joe's Pizza in Greenwich Village, where the thin, crispy crust and perfectly balanced cheese and sauce make it a favorite among locals and visitors alike, and if you're serious about your pizza, make the trip to Di Fara Pizza in Brooklyn, where each pie is handmade by Domenico DeMarco, who's been making pizza for over fifty years, and here, every slice is a work of art, with fresh ingredients and a crust that's charred just right, offering a taste that's worth the wait.

In Chinatown, you have to try the soup dumplings at Joe's Shanghai, where each dumpling is filled with savory broth and tender pork, a combination that's bursting with flavor and a must-try if you're exploring this part of the city, and don't forget to explore the area around Flushing in Queens for incredible Asian desserts, where spots like Spot Dessert Bar serve up treats like mango shaved ice and bubble tea, perfect for cooling down after a day of exploring.

Little Italy is where you'll find authentic Italian food, with Lombardi's being the go-to for coal-fired pizza, where the Margherita pizza is a classic that hasn't changed in decades, and for a more authentic experience, visit Arthur Avenue in the Bronx, known as the real Little Italy, where delis like Mike's Deli serve fresh mozzarella and prosciutto that's as good as you'll find in Italy, offering a taste of the old world right here in the city.

For fine dining, places like Le Bernardin and Eleven Madison Park set the standard, with Le Bernardin focusing on the freshest seafood, where dishes like the tuna tartare and poached lobster showcase the restaurant's commitment to excellence, and at Eleven Madison Park, the tasting menu is an adventure through flavors and textures that you won't find anywhere else, making it a dining experience that's about more than just the food—it's about creating memories.

Nightlife and Entertainment

For a night out that captures the essence of the city, you start with a Broadway show because there's nothing quite like the thrill of live theater here, and whether you go for "Hamilton" with its electrifying story and music or "The Lion King" with its stunning visuals and timeless tale, you're experiencing some of the best entertainment in the world, so if you're planning to see a show, book your tickets in advance to secure a good seat because these shows are incredibly popular, and the earlier you get your tickets, the better your options will be, and if you decide last minute, check out the TKTS booth in Times Square for discounted tickets to many shows on the day of performance.

After the show, if you're in the mood for a drink with a view, 230 Fifth is where you should go because it's one of the best rooftop bars in the city, offering incredible views of the skyline, especially of the Empire State Building, and the atmosphere here is relaxed yet vibrant, making it a perfect spot to unwind after a night at the theater, and during the colder months, you can sit inside the heated igloos and still enjoy the view without freezing, creating a unique and cozy experience that adds something special to your night.

But if you're looking for something a bit more under the radar, the speakeasy scene offers a different kind of night out, and PDT (Please Don't Tell) is one of the city's best-kept secrets because you enter through a vintage phone booth inside Crif Dogs in the East Village, leading you to an intimate, dimly lit bar that feels like you've stepped back in time, where the cocktails are expertly crafted and the vibe is cool and laid-back, making it a perfect spot if you want something quieter and more exclusive, so it's smart to make a reservation if you plan to go because the small space fills up quickly, and it's the kind of place that locals love for its atmosphere and quality.

If dancing is more your style, The Box on the Lower East Side offers a nightlife experience unlike any other, where you're not just going to a nightclub —you're stepping into a world of theatrical performances that are wild, unexpected, and sometimes shocking, and the energy here is electric, with a mix of music, dancing, and live acts that blur the lines between party and show, so it's where you go if you want a night that's anything but ordinary, giving you an experience that's immersive, high-energy, and unforgettable, and it's the kind of place that stays with you long after the night is over.

For live music, the Bowery Ballroom is where you should head because this venue is known for its incredible sound and intimate setting, making every concert feel personal and powerful, so whether you're catching an indie band on the rise or a well-known act, you'll get a night of music that's all about the connection between the artist and the audience, and it's the kind of place where music feels raw and real, making it a must-visit for any music lover who wants to experience live music the way it's meant to be heard.

If you're in the mood for comedy, the Comedy Cellar in Greenwich Village is the place to be because this legendary club is where you'll find some of the best stand-up acts in the city, often with surprise appearances by big names in comedy, and the intimate setting makes every show feel close and personal, where the laughter is nonstop and the talent on stage is top-notch, so it's the perfect way to end your night on a high note, leaving you with memories of laughter and joy that stick with you long after you've left the club.

Art, Music, and Festivals

Start with Chelsea, the core of contemporary art, where you can wander through the galleries along West 24th and West 25th Streets because this area is packed with spaces that showcase everything from avant-garde installations to striking modern paintings, and you can easily spend hours here, moving from gallery to gallery, soaking in the creativity that defines this neighborhood, so don't miss the High Line, an elevated park that not only offers beautiful views but also features rotating public art installations, providing a unique blend of nature and art in a setting that feels distinctly urban yet refreshingly open.

For live music, the Village is where you need to be, especially if you're looking for an authentic jazz experience because the Blue Note is one of the most famous jazz clubs in the world, offering a close-up view of some of the greatest jazz musicians performing in an intimate setting where every note hits just right, and it's the perfect spot to sit back with a drink and let the music take you away because the atmosphere here is as legendary as the performers who have graced its stage. If you prefer something more on the rock or indie side, the Bowery Ballroom offers an unbeatable live music experience, where the acoustics are top-notch, and the energy is palpable, making it the go-to venue for both rising stars and established bands, so whether you're here to discover new music or enjoy a performance from your favorite band, you're guaranteed a night of raw, live sound that's hard to match anywhere else.

When it comes to festivals, you can't miss the Tribeca Film Festival, which turns the city into a hub of cinematic creativity every spring because this is where independent filmmakers from around the world come to showcase their work, offering you the chance to see new films, attend panels with directors and actors, and maybe even catch a few premieres, so to get the most out of it, plan ahead, pick the films and events you're most excited about, and buy your tickets early because the most popular screenings and talks tend to sell out quickly, making this festival a must for any film lover who wants to experience the future of cinema up close.

SummerStage is another highlight, bringing free concerts to parks across the city, with Central Park being the main venue, and this festival offers an incredible range of music, from hip-hop and R&B to classical and world music, so there's always something happening, and it's one of the best ways to enjoy live performances outdoors, surrounded by the beauty of the park, so check the schedule in advance, find a concert that interests you, and plan to arrive early because these events draw big crowds, and getting a good spot can make all the difference in your experience, turning a simple concert into a memorable evening under the stars.

For art enthusiasts, the Armory Show in the fall is a must-attend event, showcasing some of the best modern and contemporary art from galleries around the world, and this isn't just an art fair—it's a chance to see ground-breaking works, meet artists and curators, and even purchase pieces if you're a collector, so make your way to the Javits Center, where the event is held, and take your time exploring the exhibits because there's always something new and exciting to discover, offering a deep dive into the trends and movements that are shaping the art world today.

If you're looking for something vibrant and full of life, the West Indian Day Parade in Brooklyn on Labor Day is an event you can't miss, where Eastern Parkway transforms into a colorful celebration of Caribbean culture, with music, dancing, and food that bring the streets to life, so get there early, wear something comfortable, and be ready to dance because this parade is all about joy and celebration, giving you a firsthand experience of the city's incredible cultural diversity in one of its most lively and energetic forms, making it a day that's filled with music, color, and the kind of excitement that only a festival like this can offer.

CHAPTER 7
ESCAPE TO NATURE

Central Park: An Urban Oasis

Central Park is where you escape the city's chaos, finding peace and nature all in one place, so start at The Mall, where the trees create a shaded walkway perfect for a long, slow stroll, especially in spring and fall when the colors change, offering you a tranquil setting right in the heart of everything, and it's the spot to clear your mind and enjoy some quiet time without leaving the city behind.

For pure relaxation, Sheep Meadow is your go-to, where you can stretch out on the grass, enjoy a picnic, or just soak up the sun, and this wide-open space gives you a break from the city streets, surrounded by others who are just here to unwind, making it an ideal spot for those lazy afternoons when you want to do nothing but relax and take in the good vibes around you, all while feeling miles away from the hustle.

If you're in the mood for a little adventure, head straight to the Ramble because this part of the park is like stepping into a forest, with winding paths that lead you through dense trees and along quiet streams, offering a real sense of exploration without ever leaving the city, so it's perfect if you want to find a secluded spot to think, read, or just enjoy the sounds of nature all around you, and it's especially beautiful in the fall when the leaves turn into a brilliant display of reds and oranges.

During summer, nothing beats renting a rowboat at the Loeb Boathouse and spending some time on the lake, where you can paddle around, enjoy the peaceful water, and maybe spot a few turtles sunning themselves because this is a unique way to see the park from the water, surrounded by the natural beauty that makes this place special, and it's an experience that feels both relaxing and refreshing, giving you a break from the heat of the city streets.

Winter turns Central Park into a snowy wonderland, and ice skating at Wollman Rink is a must-do, where you can glide across the ice with the city skyline as your backdrop, creating a perfect winter scene that feels almost magical, so bundle up and enjoy the crisp air as you skate because it's one of those classic winter activities that makes you appreciate the season in a whole new way, offering a serene yet exhilarating experience right in the middle of the city.

In spring, the cherry blossoms around the Reservoir are a sight you can't miss, turning the area into a pink paradise that's ideal for a walk or run, and the air is filled with the fresh scent of blooming flowers, making it the perfect time to explore this part of the park, so take your time to enjoy the beauty around you, and if you're into birdwatching, the Ramble is the place to be during this season, where you can spot migratory birds that pass through, offering a unique glimpse into nature right in the city's center.

Central Park isn't just a park—it's your sanctuary, a place to relax, explore, and reconnect with nature no matter the time of year, so whether you're strolling through The Mall, lounging in Sheep Meadow, wandering the Ramble, rowing on the lake, skating in winter, or enjoying the spring blooms, you're experiencing the best of what this urban oasis has to offer, and the key is to take your time, explore at your own pace, and let the park show you its beauty because every visit here is a chance to escape and find a little peace in the middle of it all.

Beyond the City: Day Trips and Nature Escapes

When you need a break from the city, head to the Hamptons for a day at the beach, where you can relax on soft, sandy shores and enjoy the ocean breeze, and Coopers Beach in Southampton is one of the best spots, offering wide stretches of sand and calm waters, perfect for a peaceful day by the sea, and Montauk's Ditch Plains Beach is ideal if you're looking for something a bit more active, especially if you're into surfing because the waves here are some of the best in the area, giving you a chance to catch a few while enjoying the laid-back vibe of this beach town. The summer is the best time to visit, but even in the off-season, the Hamptons offer a quiet escape with charming villages and beautiful coastal scenery, so pack your beach essentials and get ready for a day of sun, surf, and relaxation, just a short drive from the city.

If you prefer the mountains, the Catskills are perfect for hiking, especially the trail to Kaaterskill Falls, which is one of the tallest waterfalls in the state, offering a stunning view that makes the hike well worth it, so wear sturdy hiking shoes and bring plenty of water because the trail can be steep and rocky, but the reward at the end is a breathtaking waterfall that cascades down into a serene pool, surrounded by lush forest, creating a perfect spot to take a break and enjoy the natural beauty around you, and if you have time, explore some of the other trails in the area because the Catskills are full of hidden gems just waiting to be discovered.

For a mix of outdoor adventure and cultural experiences, head to the Hudson Valley, where you can visit the Storm King Art Center, an outdoor sculpture park that's unlike anything else, with massive works of art set against the backdrop of rolling hills and open fields, so take your time wandering through the park because every turn reveals something new and exciting, whether it's a towering sculpture or a peaceful spot to sit and take in the view. Afterward, drive along the scenic roads that wind through the valley, passing through towns like Cold Spring and Beacon, where you can stop for a bite to eat or browse local shops and galleries, offering a relaxing end to your day surrounded by the natural beauty and charm of the Hudson Valley, which is especially stunning in the fall when the leaves turn vibrant shades of red and gold, making it the perfect time to explore the area.

If you visit in the winter, the Catskills offer some of the best skiing and snowboarding in the state, with resorts like Hunter and Windham Mountain providing well-groomed trails and beautiful views, so whether you're a seasoned skier or just looking to try something new, these mountains are a winter wonderland that's just a short drive from the city, giving you a chance to enjoy the snow and the serenity of the mountains in a way that's both exciting and relaxing.

When planning your trip, think about what you want to do and pack accordingly, so for the beach, bring sunscreen, a towel, and maybe a good book to enjoy while you relax by the water, and for hiking, wear layers, bring a map or download one on your phone, and pack snacks and water to keep you energized on the trail because being prepared will make your day trip more enjoyable and allow you to focus on the experience, whether it's catching waves, hiking to a waterfall, or exploring art in the Hudson Valley.

These day trips offer the perfect escape from the city, giving you a chance to relax, recharge, and reconnect with nature, so whether you're heading to the

Hamptons, the Catskills, or the Hudson Valley, you're in for a day of adventure and beauty that's just a short drive away, offering you the perfect way to get away from it all without going too far, making your time outside the city as refreshing and rewarding as possible.

CHAPTER 8
SHOPPING IN THE BIG APPLE

Fifth Avenue and Luxury Shopping

F ifth Avenue is the ultimate destination for luxury shopping, where you're surrounded by some of the most prestigious brands and designer boutiques in the world, so start at Saks Fifth Avenue, a cornerstone of luxury, where you'll find an incredible range of designer clothing, accessories, and beauty products across its ten floors, and don't miss the famous shoe department, a haven for anyone who loves fashion, offering everything from classic styles to the latest trends, making it easy to lose yourself in the sheer variety of choices available, so if you're looking to treat yourself, this is the place to do it.

As you continue your shopping journey, Tiffany & Co. is where you go for timeless elegance and fine jewelry, where stepping into the flagship store is like entering a world of sparkle and sophistication, where you can find the perfect piece to mark a special occasion or simply admire the exquisite craftsmanship on display, so whether you're purchasing or just browsing, the experience here is all about luxury, with every corner of the store radiating class and style.

Bergdorf Goodman is another essential stop, offering a curated selection of the most exclusive designer fashion, and this store is a favorite among the fashion elite for a reason, where you'll discover couture pieces that are both unique and breathtaking, and the service here is impeccable, making your shopping experience feel personalized and luxurious, so if you're serious about high fashion, Bergdorf's is where you'll find the latest collections from the world's top designers, all in one place, and it's also home to an impressive beauty department, where you can indulge in high-end cosmetics and skincare, ensuring you leave looking and feeling your best.

For something more exclusive, explore the boutiques on Madison Avenue, where stores like The Row and Carolina Herrera offer a more intimate shopping experience, providing access to unique, high-end pieces that are hard to find elsewhere, so if you're in search of something truly special, this is where you go to find it, and the personalized service in these boutiques ensures that your shopping experience is tailored to your needs, making it feel like you're receiving the VIP treatment every step of the way.

To make the most of your visit, it's best to shop in the morning or during weekdays when the crowds are lighter, giving you more space and time to enjoy the experience because weekends, particularly during the holiday season, can be hectic, but they also offer the chance to see the famous window displays that turn shopping into a holiday spectacle, with stores like Saks and Bergdorf's creating elaborate displays that draw visitors from all over, adding a magical touch to your shopping trip and making it a memorable part of your visit to Fifth Avenue.

Fifth Avenue isn't just about shopping—it's about experiencing the pinnacle of luxury and fashion, where every store offers something unique, and every purchase feels like an investment in quality and style, so whether you're looking for the perfect gift, a statement piece for your wardrobe, or simply a day of indulgence, you'll find it here, in one of the most iconic shopping destinations in the world, where the combination of elegance, sophistication, and world-class service makes every moment special, ensuring that your time on Fifth Avenue is as enjoyable as it is memorable.

Unique Boutiques and Vintage Shops

When you're looking for unique and trendy shopping experiences, head straight to SoHo, where the boutiques are anything but ordinary, and you'll find stores like Opening Ceremony offering a mix of designer collaborations and emerging brands that you won't see anywhere else, and this is the place to find bold, statement pieces that stand out, so if you're after something that breaks away from the mainstream, this is where you start, and the best part is, everything here feels carefully curated, giving you access to the latest trends and the cutting edge of fashion, all in one place.

For vintage finds, make your way to the East Village, where stores like L Train Vintage are packed with treasures from decades past, offering everything from classic denim to vintage tees at prices that make it easy to walk away with something special, and the key here is to take your time digging through the racks because the best pieces aren't always obvious at first glance, but when you find that perfect leather jacket or a pair of retro boots, it's all worth it because these are the kinds of items that add character to your wardrobe, with each piece telling its own story, and the thrill of discovery is what makes vintage shopping so addictive.

In Williamsburg, Brooklyn, the vibe is all about individuality, and Beacon's Closet is a must-visit for anyone who loves vintage, where you can find a carefully curated selection that includes everything from high-end designer pieces to quirky, one-of-a-kind finds, and what's great about this store is the constantly changing inventory, which means every visit offers something new, so whether you're hunting for a vintage dress, a unique accessory, or just something that feels different from what everyone else is wearing, this is where you'll find it, and it's the kind of place where fashion meets sustainability, making it a top spot for those who value both style and eco-conscious shopping.

If you're after truly unique items, explore the boutiques in Nolita and the Lower East Side, where small, independent shops like Love Adorned offer a mix of handcrafted jewelry, home goods, and accessories that you won't find in larger stores, and these boutiques are perfect for discovering special pieces that have a personal touch, whether you're looking for a meaningful gift or something to add to your own collection, and the atmosphere in these neighborhoods is as eclectic as the items you'll find, with each store offering a unique blend of style, craftsmanship, and creativity that makes shopping here feel like a real adventure.

To get the best deals, shop early in the day when the stores are quieter, giving you first access to new arrivals and more time to browse without the rush, and if you're into vintage, ask the staff about restock days because that's when you'll find the freshest selections, and for boutiques, keep an eye out for end-of-season sales, where you can score high-quality items at a fraction of the original price, and don't hesitate to ask if there are any upcoming promotions or events because these stores often offer special deals that aren't widely advertised, giving you the chance to save while still getting something unique and high-quality.

Shopping in these unique boutiques and vintage stores is about more than just buying clothes—it's about finding pieces that reflect your personality and style in a way that's creative and authentic, so whether you're in SoHo for the latest trends, the East Village for vintage treasures, or Williamsburg for something truly different, each item you find will be a reminder of the city's vibrant, creative energy, and the key is to enjoy the hunt, embrace the unexpected, and leave with something that's not just an item of clothing, but a piece of the city itself, ready to be woven into your own story.

Local Markets and Artisan Crafts

For a true taste of the city's creativity, you need to visit Chelsea Market because it's more than just a shopping destination—it's a vibrant hub where you can find some of the best artisanal vendors offering everything from gourmet foods to handcrafted goods, and when you walk through those doors, the first thing you'll notice is the smell of fresh bread and coffee, but take your time because as you move deeper into the market, you'll discover unique shops selling hand-made jewelry, one-of-a-kind ceramics, and specialty items that make perfect souvenirs or gifts, and the best time to visit is early in the morning before the crowds arrive, giving you the space to explore at your own pace, savoring each discovery as you go because this is the kind of place where every corner has something worth seeing, tasting, or buying.

If you're interested in experiencing the city's diverse culture through its markets, then Union Square Greenmarket is where you need to be, and this market is famous for bringing together local farmers and artisans who sell fresh, organic produce, artisanal breads, and handcrafted items that are as unique as they are high-quality, so visit on a Wednesday or Saturday when the market is at its busiest, with the widest variety of vendors, and take your time to talk with them, ask questions, and learn about the products because the connections you make here are part of what makes this market so special, giving you an authentic farm-to-table experience right in the heart of the city, and it's not just about buying—it's about connecting with the people behind the products, who are passionate about what they do and more than willing to share their stories with you.

When it comes to finding truly unique pieces, Artists & Fleas in Williamsburg is unbeatable because it's where local designers, artists, and vintage collectors come together to offer a mix of products you won't find anywhere else, and as you walk through, you'll see everything from vintage clothing and handmade jewelry to original artwork and custom furniture, and the vibe is all about discovery, so plan your visit for the weekend when the market is in full swing, and make sure to arrive early for the best selection because the variety here is endless, and the thrill of finding that perfect item—whether it's a vintage leather jacket or a piece of handcrafted jewelry—makes the experience feel more like a treasure hunt than just another shopping trip, and every piece you buy here feels like a special find, something that reflects your personal style and the creative spirit of the city.

If you love the charm of a classic flea market, Brooklyn Flea is where you'll find the best mix of antiques, vintage items, and handmade crafts, making it the perfect place to spend a day hunting for unique finds, and the market is famous for offering everything from mid-century furniture and retro clothing to rare vinyl records and beautifully crafted jewelry, so arrive early for the best selection and be ready to haggle a bit because part of the fun here is negotiating with vendors to get the best deal, and don't miss out on the food vendors scattered throughout the market, offering artisanal treats that are as delicious as they are unique, giving you the chance to grab a bite while you shop.

For a market experience that supports local artisans and gives you the chance to bring home something truly unique, Grand Bazaar NYC on the Upper West Side is the place to go because this market is all about showcasing the best of local craftsmanship, with vendors offering everything from handcrafted jewelry and artisanal foods to unique vintage finds, and the market takes place every Sunday, rain or shine, making it the perfect way to spend a weekend morning exploring what the city's most creative minds have to offer, and since all proceeds from the market go to supporting local schools, shopping here isn't just about buying something special—it's about giving back to the community and supporting the people who make this city so vibrant and creative, making it a must-visit for anyone looking to experience the true spirit of the city through its markets and the people who bring them to life.

These markets are more than just places to shop—they're where you connect with the heart and soul of the city, so whether you're after handmade crafts, artisanal foods, or something completely unique, each of these markets offers an experience that goes beyond buying—it's about discovering, connecting, and taking a piece of the city home with you, and the key is to explore with an open mind, take your time, and enjoy every moment because you never know what you'll find, and that's what makes shopping in these markets so special.

CHAPTER 9
PRACTICAL TIPS FOR A
SMOOTH TRIP

Staying Safe in the City

To stay safe in the city, keep your belongings secure and stay aware of your surroundings, especially in crowded places like busy streets and subway stations because these are spots where pickpockets often operate, so it's essential to keep your bag in front of you, zipped up, and within your sight at all times, making it hard for anyone to reach in without you noticing, and if you carry a wallet, put it in your front pocket or a secure spot that's difficult for anyone to access easily, because this small step can save you from a lot of trouble later.

When walking around, stay focused on what's happening around you, and avoid distractions like constantly checking your phone while you're moving because this not only makes you less aware of your surroundings but also signals to others that you're not paying attention, so if you need to look at a map or directions, stop to the side where you can safely check without blocking the flow of foot traffic or exposing yourself to unnecessary risk, which keeps you safer and helps you stay connected to what's going on around you.

Cross streets carefully because traffic can be unpredictable, with cars, bikes, and taxis moving quickly, so always cross at designated crosswalks and wait for the light to change, even if it feels like everyone else is rushing ahead because taking those extra seconds to make sure it's safe is worth it, and be particularly careful at intersections where cars might be turning, as drivers are often more focused on other vehicles than on pedestrians, making it crucial for you to stay alert and ensure they see you before stepping into the street.

When it comes to managing your money, try to use a credit or debit card as much as possible to avoid carrying too much cash, and if you do need cash, only take out what you need for the day and store it in a secure place, preferably in a money belt or a hidden pocket that's not easily accessible to others, and when using an ATM, choose one that's inside a bank or a well-populated area to reduce the risk of theft or unwanted attention because it's all about minimizing the chances of anything going wrong by making smart, simple choices that keep you safe.

If you ever feel uncomfortable or unsafe, whether someone is too close for comfort on the subway or you sense that you're being followed, trust your instincts and act immediately by moving to a crowded area, entering a nearby store, or finding a police officer or security guard because the sooner you change your environment or seek help, the better, and never hesitate to ask for assistance if you feel you need it because the city is full of people who can help, and it's always better to be cautious and proactive rather than ignore your gut feeling, which can often alert you to something before it becomes a problem.

Preparation is important, so keep a list of emergency contacts on your phone, including local police, your hotel, and anyone you're traveling with, and always carry a portable charger to ensure your phone stays powered throughout the day because being able to reach out for help or find your way back if you're lost is key to staying safe, and knowing you have a way to connect gives you peace of mind, allowing you to enjoy your trip without unnecessary worry.

By staying alert, securing your belongings, and making smart decisions, you can explore the city with confidence, knowing that you've taken the necessary steps to protect yourself, so enjoy your trip, keep these tips in mind, and focus on making the most of your time in the city, where you can experience everything it has to offer without compromising your safety.

Tipping and Service Etiquette

When you're dining out, tipping 15% to 20% of the total bill is standard, and you should aim for 20% if the service is good because that's what's expected here, so when the check comes, just take the total amount, move the decimal one place to the left to get 10%, then double that number for an easy 20% tip because this simple method makes it quick and straightforward, and always remember that this tip is a direct reflection of the service, not the food itself, so even if the meal isn't perfect, if your server did a good job, they should get the full tip they deserve.

In taxis, tipping around 15% to 20% of the fare is typical, and if the driver helps with your bags, takes a quick route, or is particularly friendly, consider tipping a little extra to show your appreciation because cab drivers rely heavily on tips as part of their income, and being generous when the service is good is a way to recognize their efforts, plus, if you're using a ride-hailing app, it often gives you an option to add a tip directly, which simplifies the process and ensures the driver is compensated fairly for their service.

When you're at a hotel, tipping varies depending on the service you receive, so for the bellhop who helps with your luggage, tipping $1 to $2 per bag is standard, more if they're heavy or if the service was particularly prompt, and for housekeeping, it's good practice to leave $2 to $5 per night, depending on the service and the condition of the room when you leave it, and always place the tip on the pillow or in a clearly marked envelope to ensure it's recognized as a tip, which makes it clear and appreciated, and if you order room service, check the bill first to see if gratuity is included, then add 15% to 20% if it's not because that's the norm for good service, and it avoids any confusion about whether or not you've tipped appropriately.

For counter-service spots, like coffee shops, it's polite to leave some change or round up to the nearest dollar, especially if the service is quick and friendly because even though tipping here isn't mandatory, it's a nice gesture and shows that you appreciate the effort, and you'll often see a tip jar or have the option to add a tip when paying by card, so just drop in some change or select a small amount on the screen to show your appreciation, and when it comes to delivery drivers, tipping at least $2 to $5 is standard, with more for larger orders or bad weather, because they've gone out of their way to bring your order to you, and tipping generously here is a way to acknowledge their effort and ensure they're fairly compensated.

At bars, tipping is simple—$1 to $2 per drink, depending on what you order, is expected, with $1 for a beer and $2 for a cocktail, and if you're running a tab, tipping 15% to 20% at the end of the night is standard, making it easier than tipping for each drink individually, and remember, bartenders often reward good tippers with quicker service and even the occasional free drink, so it pays off to be generous if you plan on visiting the same spot more than once during your trip.

Knowing how and when to tip in these situations helps you navigate the city with confidence, ensuring you always show appreciation for good service, and by following these straightforward guidelines, you'll avoid any awkward moments and contribute to the livelihoods of those who work hard to make your experience enjoyable, so keep these tips in mind as you explore, and you'll always be prepared to tip appropriately, making your trip smoother and more enjoyable for everyone involved.

Dealing with Crowds and Peak Times

To make your visit smoother and avoid the frustration of heavy crowds, you need to be smart about timing and location, so if you're planning to visit popular attractions like the Empire State Building or the Statue of Liberty, arrive early when they open or late in the afternoon when the crowds are thinner because this way, you'll spend less time waiting in lines and more time actually enjoying what you came to see, and the experience becomes more personal and less rushed, allowing you to take in the views and atmosphere without feeling overwhelmed by other tourists.

When you're walking through crowded areas like Times Square or Fifth Avenue, stick to the right side of the sidewalk and move with the flow because this helps you avoid bumping into people and keeps you moving at a steady pace, so if you need to stop, step aside near a building or shop front to avoid blocking the path, which not only keeps the crowd flowing but also gives you a moment to get your bearings or snap a quick photo without feeling pressured by the people around you, and during rush hours, it's best to avoid the busiest streets and use quieter side streets to get where you're going more easily and with less stress.

For a break from the hustle, find quieter spots like the northern parts of Central Park near Harlem Meer or the Ramble, where you can relax away from the usual tourist crowds and enjoy some peace in the middle of the city, and if you're in Midtown, head to Bryant Park early in the day when it's less busy, so you can sit by the fountain with a coffee and enjoy a calm moment before diving back into your day, and Washington Square Park is another great choice for a quieter atmosphere, especially in the early afternoon, where you can watch the city go by without the usual rush of people around you.

If you want to visit museums without the crowds, go on weekdays in the late afternoon when most tourists and school groups have left, which gives you the chance to explore the exhibits at your own pace without feeling hurried, so check the museum's schedule for late openings because these are often the best times to go if you want a more relaxed visit, and if you're visiting on a weekend, buy your tickets online and arrive as soon as the museum opens, which helps you get ahead of the crowds and enjoy the exhibits with fewer people around, making your experience more enjoyable and less stressful.

Public transportation can be crowded during rush hours, so if you need to use the subway between 7:30 and 9:30 AM or 4:30 and 6:30 PM, be prepared for packed trains and busy platforms, so keep your belongings close and be ready to move quickly when entering and exiting the train, which helps you avoid getting caught in the rush of people, and if you'd rather avoid the subway during these times, consider walking or taking a taxi if your destination isn't far, which allows you to enjoy the city from above ground and avoid the stress of a crowded commute.

By planning your visits around peak times, choosing less crowded routes, and finding quieter spots to relax, you'll make your trip more enjoyable and stress-free, allowing you to experience everything the city has to offer without the frustration of dealing with large crowds, so keep these strategies in mind, and you'll navigate the city smoothly, making the most of your time here without unnecessary hassle.

Emergency Contacts and Useful Apps

Always keep these essential contacts and apps handy because they'll make your trip safer and more manageable, so first, for any emergency, dial 911 because this connects you directly to police, fire, or medical services, which is crucial if you find yourself in a serious situation, and if you need non-emergency help, like reporting a problem or getting city information, call 311 because it's the number to use for all sorts of city services, making it a reliable go-to when you need assistance that isn't life-threatening, and for medical care, Mount Sinai Hospital at 212-241-6500 and NYU Langone Health at 212-263-7300 are top facilities that you can trust if you need medical attention, so having these numbers saved ensures you're prepared for anything.

When it comes to getting around, you'll want Google Maps on your phone because it's the best app for finding directions, whether you're walking, taking the subway, or driving, and it shows real-time updates on traffic and transit, helping you avoid delays and get where you need to go faster, and don't forget to download maps for offline use, which is really useful if you're in an area with spotty reception, so this way, you'll always know where you're going, even without a signal, which is especially important in a big city where getting lost can be stressful.

For public transportation, Citymapper is the app you need because it's specifically designed to help you navigate the subway, buses, and even walking routes, with real-time updates that let you know if there are any service changes or delays, so you can adjust your plans on the go and avoid getting stuck, and MyMTA is another essential app because it gives you live updates for subway and bus services, making it easy to plan your trips with accurate, up-to-the-minute information, which is crucial for staying on schedule in a city where timing can make all the difference.

If you're traveling internationally or find yourself in a neighborhood where English isn't the first language, Google Translate is a must because it can translate text, voice, and even images instantly, which is perfect for reading signs, menus, or communicating with locals when language barriers might otherwise slow you down, so having this app ready to go ensures you can keep moving smoothly without misunderstanding or frustration, making it easier to enjoy every part of the city, no matter where you are or what language you encounter.

When it comes to finding the best places to eat, shop, or explore, Yelp is your go-to app because it provides real user reviews and ratings that help you choose wisely, so whether you're looking for a great restaurant, a unique shop, or just want to see what's nearby, Yelp gives you all the details you need to make an informed decision, which is especially helpful in a city where there's so much to see and do, and you want to make sure you're choosing the best options for your time and money.

By keeping these contacts saved and these apps downloaded, you'll be well-equipped to handle anything the city throws your way, ensuring that you're prepared, informed, and ready to enjoy your trip without unnecessary stress, so take the time to set up your phone with these tools because they'll make all the difference, helping you navigate the city confidently, find help when you need it, and make the most of every moment you spend exploring.

Handling Unexpected Situations

If your luggage doesn't show up, go straight to the airline's lost luggage counter because you need to file a report immediately, so make sure you have your baggage claim ticket ready, and be clear when describing your bags, then leave your contact details so they can reach you as soon as your luggage is found because this will speed up the process of getting your things back, and always pack a change of clothes and essential items like medications in your carry-on to avoid being caught completely unprepared while you wait for your luggage to be returned to you.

When the weather changes suddenly, you need to adjust quickly by switching to indoor activities like visiting a museum, catching a show, or exploring indoor markets because these options keep you comfortable and still allow you to make the most of your day, and always carry an umbrella or a light rain jacket in your bag, which helps you stay dry and keeps the weather from ruining your plans altogether.

If you miss a reservation, call the restaurant immediately to let them know because they might hold your table or offer a later time, and if they can't accommodate you, ask for recommendations nearby since many restaurants are connected to others in the area, and they can point you in the right direction so your evening doesn't go to waste, and keep apps like OpenTable handy because they can help you secure a last-minute reservation somewhere else, ensuring you still have a great dining experience.

If you get lost, pull out your phone and use Google Maps to find your way, and if your battery is low, step into a store or café to ask for directions and charge your phone while you do because locals are usually helpful, and having a fully charged phone or a portable charger with you ensures you're never without a way to navigate, making it easier to get back on track quickly without stress.

If your plans fall through unexpectedly, like a canceled tour or a closed attraction, look for alternatives nearby using Yelp or Google Maps because this lets you find other things to do without wasting time, and being flexible means you can turn any setback into a new opportunity to explore something different, which keeps your trip exciting even when things don't go as planned, so staying adaptable is key to enjoying your trip fully, no matter what comes up.

Handling these situations calmly and efficiently will help you stay in control and make the most of your visit, so being prepared and flexible is the best way to ensure that unexpected changes don't ruin your experience but instead become just another part of your adventure.

CHAPTER 10
STEP-BY-STEP GUIDES AND ITINERARIES

One-Day Itinerary: NYC Highlights

S tart your day with the first ferry to the Statue of Liberty from Battery Park because getting there early means fewer crowds and more time to explore, and make sure you've booked tickets for the pedestal or crown ahead of time if you want those amazing views from above, because once you're on Liberty Island, take your time walking around, absorbing the history, and checking out the museum, which gives you a real sense of the city's beginnings and the symbol of freedom that's recognized around the world, and this experience sets the stage perfectly for your day, giving you that feeling of connection to something bigger right from the start.

After you're done, head straight to the 9/11 Memorial and Museum because this site is not just about seeing—it's about feeling, and spend a few moments by the memorial pools, which are a powerful tribute to those lost, then go inside the museum to understand the impact of that day, and it's not just a visit but a moment of reflection and a way to connect deeply with the city's story of resilience and recovery, so when you finish, take a moment to look up at One World Trade Center because it's more than just a building—it's a statement of strength, and if time allows, visiting the observation deck is worth it for a stunning view of the city from the top.

Next, make your way uptown to the Empire State Building because this isn't just a skyscraper—it's a piece of the city's soul, so head up to the 86th floor for views that go on forever, and from up here, you'll really see how massive the city is, with the grid of streets below and the rivers framing the skyline, and it's not just about the view but also the feeling of standing in a place that's been a part of so many stories, movies, and moments in history, and when you're ready, a quick walk or subway ride will get you to your next stop without missing a beat.

Now it's time to slow down a little in Central Park because after all that high energy, a stroll through the park's greenery is exactly what you need, so wander through Bethesda Terrace, cross the Bow Bridge, and find your way to the quiet of Strawberry Fields, where you can sit and take it all in, and whether you're walking, biking, or just sitting on a bench, Central Park gives you a chance to breathe and see the city from a different perspective, where nature and urban life blend together perfectly, giving you that unique city-meets-nature vibe that you can't get anywhere else.

After your park visit, head to the Metropolitan Museum of Art because you're not just looking at art—you're stepping into history, culture, and creativity from every corner of the world, so hit the must-sees like the Egyptian Temple of Dendur, the European paintings, and the American Wing, and don't skip the rooftop if it's open because the views over the park and city are another layer to this experience, and with so much to see, it's all about picking your favorites and making the most of the time you have without trying to take in every single piece, which can be overwhelming, so stick to what grabs your interest and enjoy it fully.

End your day in Times Square because this is where the city's pulse really beats—bright lights, constant motion, and that electric feeling that you're in the center of it all, so take in the billboards, the crowds, and the energy that makes this spot so famous, and whether you're grabbing dinner nearby, catching a Broadway show, or just standing in the middle of it all, Times Square is the perfect cap to a day of exploring the city's highlights, giving you that final burst of excitement and a sense of having seen the very heart of the city before you wrap up your one-day adventure.

This one-day itinerary captures the essence of the city, hitting all the iconic spots with just the right mix of sightseeing, culture, and local flavor, so you'll end your day feeling like you've truly experienced what the city is all about, even if your time here is short.

Three-Day Itinerary: A Balanced Tour

Day One: Get an early start and take the first ferry to the Statue of Liberty and Ellis Island because you want to avoid the crowds and really take your time here—reserve pedestal or crown tickets in advance for that extra view, and after exploring the museum on Ellis Island, which dives deep into the stories of immigrants who passed through, grab a quick bite from a food cart at Battery Park to keep moving, then walk over to the 9/11 Memorial and Museum because this place hits hard, but it's essential to understand the impact and resilience of the city, so take a moment at the reflecting pools, then head inside to see the artifacts and stories that bring the events to life, and if you're feeling up for it, go to the One World Observatory for sweeping city views, which kind of puts everything in perspective.

Make your way uptown to the Empire State Building because no trip is complete without seeing the city from up high, and the 86th-floor observation deck offers incredible views that stretch as far as the eye can see, so after you've soaked in the sights, grab a coffee nearby and walk over to Bryant Park, which is like a little oasis where you can relax, sit on the lawn, or just watch the world go by, and it's perfect for a quick recharge before heading to Times Square as the sun sets because this place is pure energy with its neon lights, buzzing crowds, and that sense of being at the center of it all, so take your time here, explore, and if you've got tickets to a Broadway show, this is the perfect time to catch it, or just find a spot to eat nearby where you can soak in the city vibes.

Day Two: Start your morning with a walk or bike ride through Central Park because it's the city's best way to unwind, with paths that lead you to iconic spots like Bethesda Terrace, the Bow Bridge, and Strawberry Fields, and if you're up for something active, rent a rowboat at the Loeb Boathouse because it's a peaceful way to take in the park from the water, and after exploring, head to the Metropolitan Museum of Art, where you should zero in on the highlights like the Egyptian Temple of Dendur, the European galleries, and the rooftop garden for views that mix art with skyline, so grab a map, pick your favorites, and dive in without feeling like you have to see it all because it's huge and can easily take a whole day.

Spend the afternoon strolling down Fifth Avenue because this is shopping central, even if you're just window-shopping, and check out places like Saks Fifth Avenue, the Apple Store, or even just admire the architecture as you walk, and from there, make your way to Rockefeller Center to go up to Top of the Rock because the views here, especially at sunset, are unbeatable—you'll see the Empire State Building, Central Park, and everything in between, so take your time up there, then head down to explore the plaza below, which is lively and full of shops, ice skating in winter, or outdoor dining in summer, making it a perfect spot to wrap up the afternoon, and end your day with dinner in Hell's Kitchen, where you'll find tons of great restaurants from every cuisine imaginable, so just pick a spot that catches your eye and enjoy a good meal.

Day Three: Dive into the neighborhoods today, starting with SoHo because this is where you'll find cool boutiques, art galleries, and that trendy vibe that makes it fun to just wander without a plan, so take your time, browse around, grab a coffee, and enjoy the street art, then head to the Lower East Side to visit the Tenement Museum, which is unlike any other museum because it takes you inside the apartments of immigrants who lived here, showing you the real, gritty history of the city in a personal way, and after the museum, grab a quick lunch at one of the nearby delis or cafes because this area is known for its food scene, offering everything from classic bagels to modern vegan spots, so there's something for everyone.

Cross into Brooklyn by walking the Brooklyn Bridge because this isn't just a way to get from A to B—it's an experience, with views of the skyline that are perfect for photos, and once you're in Brooklyn, spend some time in DUMBO, exploring the waterfront, checking out Jane's Carousel, or just enjoying the street vibe, then grab a slice of pizza at Juliana's or Grimaldi's because you can't go wrong with either, and after lunch, head to Williamsburg to explore the shops, markets, and street art that make this neighborhood feel like a city within a city, full of creativity and local flavor, so take it slow, enjoy the atmosphere, and maybe pick up a unique souvenir or two.

Finish your day back in Manhattan with a sunset walk along the High Line because this elevated park gives you a unique view of the city from above the streets, lined with art installations, gardens, and benches where you can sit and just take it all in, and as the sun sets, the lights of the city start to glow, creating a magical end to your day, so once you've walked the High Line, head to Chelsea Market for dinner because this place is a foodie's paradise with so many options under one roof, from seafood to tacos to desserts, making it the perfect spot to grab a casual, delicious meal and reflect on all the amazing sights you've seen over these three packed days.

This three-day plan balances the city's top landmarks, cultural insights, and neighborhood vibes, giving you a true feel of the city from every angle, making sure you leave with a well-rounded experience that captures the heart and soul of the city without feeling rushed or overwhelmed.

One-Week Itinerary: In-Depth Exploration

Day One: Start with the ferry to the Statue of Liberty and Ellis Island early— get the first ferry out of Battery Park around 8:30 AM because it's quieter and you'll have more time to explore, and take your time with the exhibits at Ellis Island, where the history is rich and the stories of immigrants are powerful, then grab a quick bite at Battery Park—nothing fancy, just something to keep you going, like a hot dog or pretzel from a cart, and head straight to the 9/11 Memorial and Museum because it's essential to see and really understand the impact of that day, and spend some time at the reflecting pools, then dive into the museum's detailed exhibits which will guide you through the events with a mix of personal stories, artifacts, and visuals that hit hard but are worth it, and after, go up to One World Observatory because it's the perfect way to orient yourself with the city from above, offering views that stretch for miles, letting you pinpoint places you'll explore later in the week.

Day Two: Start at the Empire State Building first thing in the morning around 8 AM so you can get up to the 86th-floor observation deck without too much of a wait, and from there, head over to Bryant Park for breakfast in the park—grab something from a nearby café and enjoy it on the green tables as you watch the city start to wake up, and take a quick peek inside the New York Public Library next door because the architecture alone is worth a look, even if you're not there to read, then stroll to Grand Central Terminal where you can marvel at the ceiling's constellations and the busy but organized chaos of commuters and tourists alike, and maybe grab a snack or a coffee from the food market inside, and after that, walk to the Museum of Modern Art, focusing on iconic pieces like Van Gogh's Starry Night or Warhol's Campbell's Soup Cans, then spend some time on Fifth Avenue for shopping or just window browsing —places like Saks, Tiffany's, and the massive Apple Store are worth checking out, even if just for the displays, and end your day at Top of the Rock at Rockefeller Center, aiming for sunset when the city lights start to glow, giving you stunning views of both the Empire State Building and Central Park all in one sweeping vista.

Day Three: Dedicate this day to Central Park and its surroundings, starting with a relaxed walk through the park's southeast entrance at 59th Street and Central Park West, making your way to spots like Bethesda Terrace, Bow Bridge, and the Alice in Wonderland statue, because these are must-see highlights that offer beautiful photo ops and a real sense of what makes the park special, then visit the Metropolitan Museum of Art, but don't try to see everything because it's huge—focus on the Egyptian Wing, the European Paintings, and the American Art sections, and definitely hit the rooftop for some fresh air and city views, and if you're hungry, grab a quick lunch from a food cart or a nearby deli and have a picnic in the park, enjoying a laid-back meal surrounded by locals and tourists alike, and after lunch, wander through the Upper East Side, where you can check out the beautiful brownstones, boutique shops, and maybe pop into the Guggenheim if you're up for more art, or just keep it light with some window shopping and a coffee stop.

Day Four: Head downtown to Greenwich Village in the morning because this neighborhood is all about exploring at your own pace—start at Washington Square Park where you can see the iconic arch, watch musicians and artists, and feel the creative energy that defines this area, then wander through the Village's narrow streets, stopping at quirky shops, cozy cafes, and spots like Café Wha? where music legends once played, and keep walking south into SoHo where you'll find cobblestone streets, high-end boutiques, and a mix of art galleries and pop-up shops that keep the area buzzing with activity, so take your time browsing, enjoy the window displays, and maybe grab a treat from a local bakery like Dominique Ansel, home of the cronut, then head over to the Lower East Side to visit the Tenement Museum because this place offers a unique, intimate look at the lives of the immigrants who built the city, and it's not just a museum—it's an experience that makes history feel real and personal, then wrap up your day with dinner in the East Village, where the options are endless, from classic ramen at Ippudo to vegan delights at Superiority Burger, and maybe finish with a drink at one of the neighborhood's cool bars or speakeasies, where the vibe is always laid-back and welcoming.

Day Five: Start your Brooklyn day with a walk across the Brooklyn Bridge because this isn't just a crossing—it's a moment to take in the skyline and snap some of the best photos of the trip, and once you're in DUMBO, explore the waterfront parks, take that classic photo of the Manhattan Bridge with the Empire State Building framed in the arch, and grab a coffee at a local spot like Butler or a treat from Almondine, then make your way to Williamsburg, where you'll find an eclectic mix of indie shops, street art, and local designers, and if you're there on a weekend, Smorgasburg is a must because this outdoor food market is packed with vendors offering everything from gourmet donuts to ramen burgers, giving you a taste of Brooklyn's food scene in one lively spot, and spend your afternoon in Prospect Park, which has the relaxed vibe of a local hangout with sprawling green spaces, bike rentals, and a lake where you can paddle or just chill by the shore, then explore the Brooklyn Museum nearby because it offers a fantastic range of art that's often more diverse and experimental than what you'll find in Manhattan, and end your day in Park Slope, where the tree-lined streets and charming brownstones set a perfect backdrop for dinner at a neighborhood favorite like Al Di La Trattoria for authentic Italian or one of the many casual eateries offering everything from tacos to sushi.

Day Six: Explore Harlem in the morning, starting with a visit to the Apollo Theater, where the legends of music got their start—just standing outside is a moment if you're into music history, then walk along 125th Street where you can shop at local stores, grab some classic soul food at Sylvia's, or try something a bit more modern at Red Rooster, which mixes Harlem's rich history with contemporary twists, then make your way to The Bronx, beginning with the New York Botanical Garden where you can spend hours wandering through lush themed gardens, and if the Orchid Show or Holiday Train Show is on, it's a must-see, then check out the Bronx Zoo next door, which is one of the largest zoos in the country and offers a chance to see everything from big cats to gorillas, making it perfect for all ages, and cap off your Bronx trip with a visit to Arthur Avenue, known as the city's real Little Italy, where you'll find family-run restaurants serving some of the best Italian food outside of Italy itself, so sit down for a hearty pasta dish, grab a fresh pastry, or pick up some homemade mozzarella to take with you—it's all about the food here and it's as authentic as it gets.

Day Seven: Take the Staten Island Ferry for your final day, which offers stunning views of the Statue of Liberty and the Manhattan skyline for free, and once on Staten Island, visit Historic Richmond Town because this living history museum lets you step back in time with preserved buildings and reenactments that show you what life was like centuries ago, then head over to Snug Harbor Cultural Center and Botanical Garden, where you can explore multiple gardens, including a serene Chinese Scholar's Garden that feels like a world away from the busy city, and finish your day at the beaches of Staten Island, like South Beach or Midland Beach, where you can walk the boardwalk, relax on the sand, or just enjoy the sound of the waves and the sea breeze—it's a low-key way to unwind and reflect on your week, giving you a peaceful close to your deep dive into the city.

This one-week itinerary balances iconic sights, neighborhood explorations, and those local hidden gems that make the city feel personal and unique, making sure you leave feeling like you've truly lived the city, not just visited.

Themed Itineraries

For Art Lovers: Start right at The Metropolitan Museum of Art because it's not just massive; it's like stepping into different worlds—whether you're moving through ancient Egyptian temples, medieval armor, or Impressionist paintings, you're literally surrounded by some of the most important art pieces in history, so make sure you see the Temple of Dendur, which sits in its own grand hall with a reflecting pool, and take your time with the European Paintings wing where you can see works by masters like Monet, Rembrandt, and Caravaggio, and don't skip the Rooftop Garden if it's open because the views of the city are unbeatable and it's a great spot to take a breather, and once you've soaked in enough, head down Museum Mile to the Guggenheim, where the spiral design alone is worth the visit because it's a completely different experience from walking room to room, and as you wind your way up the ramp, you'll find modern and contemporary art that often surprises, challenges, or just makes you stop and think; next, make your way to MoMA because this is where you get to see Starry Night and Picasso's Les Demoiselles d'Avignon up close, plus they've got a lot of modern design and everyday objects that remind you art is everywhere, then wrap up your day at the Whitney Museum in the Meatpacking District, where American art takes the spotlight, and it's more about experiencing contemporary works that push the envelope, plus the outdoor terraces offer a unique way to view both the art inside and the city outside, which ties everything together in a way that feels like the perfect ending to a day spent deep in the art world.

For Foodies: Start your day at Chelsea Market because it's a food lover's playground with so many options, and you'll want to try a bit of everything, so go for a lobster roll at The Lobster Place, a quick taco at Los Tacos No. 1, and definitely grab some mini doughnuts at Doughnuttery because you're here to sample it all, then walk it off on the High Line—this elevated park isn't just for the views; it's lined with food vendors and art, giving you little surprises along the way, and when you're ready for lunch, hit the East Village where you've got tons of choices like Superiority Burger for creative veggie dishes or Ippudo for some seriously good ramen, and don't miss a quick stop in Chinatown for dim sum at Jing Fong or some bubble tea from Tiger Sugar because it's about sampling as much as you can in the time you have; for dinner, head over to Williamsburg in Brooklyn where the food scene is always buzzing, and if it's the weekend, you have to check out Smorgasburg, an open-air food market with over 100 vendors offering everything from gourmet donuts to fusion dishes you didn't even know you needed in your life, and if Smorgasburg isn't on, just explore the local eateries along Bedford Avenue—grab a seat at Peter Luger if you're up for a steak experience like no other, or keep it casual with Roberta's for wood-fired pizza that people line up for because it's just that good, finishing your day with a sunset view of Manhattan from one of the waterfront parks, which makes for a perfect end to a day dedicated to indulging in every bite the city has to offer.

For History Buffs: Start with the American Museum of Natural History, focusing on the Hall of Saurischian Dinosaurs where the T. rex and other massive skeletons are mind-blowing in their size and scale, but don't forget to explore the Hall of Human Origins because it gives a deep dive into our own evolutionary journey, which is fascinating to see all laid out with real fossils and artifacts, then cross Central Park to the Frick Collection on the Upper East Side, where you'll get a glimpse of life among the New York elite in the early 1900s—it's not just about the art, which is stunning, but also about the house itself, which feels like stepping back in time, and after soaking in the elegance of the Frick, make your way downtown to the Tenement Museum in the Lower East Side, where you'll get an intimate look at the lives of immigrant families who lived in these cramped apartments, and it's not just a look but an experience as you move through rooms that are preserved exactly as they were, filled with the hopes and struggles of those who passed through, and end your day at the 9/11 Memorial and Museum, which goes beyond just remembering—it's about understanding the resilience and spirit of a city that came together after tragedy, with exhibits that take you from the minute-by-minute events of the day to the global impact that followed, and walking through this space, seeing the artifacts, hearing the stories, it's a powerful way to connect with the very real and recent history that continues to shape the city today.

For Families: Start at Central Park Zoo, where you'll find everything from sea lions to penguins, and it's small enough to see everything without feeling rushed but big enough to keep everyone entertained, then head over to the Alice in Wonderland statue, where kids can climb and play while you snap some fun photos, and grab a quick snack or a full picnic in the park, because with all the open spaces and playgrounds, it's easy to find a spot to relax; from there, it's a short walk to the American Museum of Natural History, which is perfect for kids with its massive dinosaur skeletons, the life-size blue whale, and hands-on exhibits in the Discovery Room where they can touch and explore, and plan to spend a few hours because there's just so much to see, then in the afternoon, take a trip to the Children's Museum of Manhattan, which is packed with interactive exhibits that are all about learning through play, with sections dedicated to water play, arts and crafts, and even exhibits that bring favorite TV characters to life in ways that are engaging and educational; finish the day with a ride on the Staten Island Ferry, where the kids can enjoy the boat ride and views of the Statue of Liberty, and once on Staten Island, you can either hop right back or take a quick walk along the waterfront park for a chance to run around before heading back, making it a perfect low-cost way to end the day on a high note with incredible views and some fun on the water.

Off-the-Beaten-Path Itineraries

Kick off your off-the-beaten-path exploration in the East Village because it's where you'll find the city's eclectic soul without the tourist buzz, so grab a coffee from Ninth Street Espresso and head to Tompkins Square Park—this isn't just a park, it's the heart of the neighborhood with skaters, artists, and musicians creating a vibrant, lived-in energy that you'll feel the moment you step in, and as you move through the area, make sure to check out St. Mark's Place, which is packed with quirky shops like Search & Destroy where you can dig through punk rock gear and vintage treasures that scream individuality, then wander into the hidden community gardens like 6BC Garden, a real urban oasis tucked between buildings with locals tending to the plants and quiet corners perfect for a little escape from the city's pace, and when you're hungry, hit up Veselka, a neighborhood staple for Ukrainian comfort food—don't leave without trying their pierogis or a bowl of borscht, served up in a no-frills diner that's been dishing out homey meals for over half a century, giving you a taste of the East Village's rich immigrant history.

Move uptown to the Upper West Side for a quieter vibe that's full of local character, starting with the Nicholas Roerich Museum, which is a small, serene space dedicated to the works of Roerich whose colorful, mystical paintings make you feel like you've walked into a peaceful retreat, and from there, head to The Hungarian Pastry Shop, where the walls are lined with books and the air is filled with the smell of fresh pastries—order a slice of cheesecake or a strudel and settle in, because this isn't just about the food, it's about soaking in the old-world atmosphere that feels miles away from the hustle, then take a walk through Riverside Park, a less crowded but beautiful green space along the Hudson River, where the breeze off the water and the quiet paths give you a perfect spot to unwind, especially near the 79th Street Boat Basin, a hidden gem where you can watch the boats and relax without the crush of tourists, and while you're in the area, don't miss The Cathedral of St. John the Divine, a breathtakingly huge cathedral that's one of the largest in the world—step inside to marvel at the towering architecture, but also check out the tranquil garden in the back where you'll find peacocks wandering around, offering an unexpected, peaceful break right in the middle of the city.

Over in Red Hook, Brooklyn, start at Louis Valentino Jr. Pier, where you get a stunning view of the Statue of Liberty from a quiet spot that feels like a secret —this waterfront neighborhood has an industrial vibe with a creative twist, so grab a key lime pie from Steve's Authentic Key Lime Pies because it's a must-do here, and as you explore, pop into Pioneer Works, an arts and culture center housed in a massive warehouse that often has interactive exhibits, performances, and community events, all in a space that feels like it's part gallery, part playground, then unwind at Sunny's Bar, a legendary dive bar that's been around since the 1890s with a cozy, unpretentious feel and often has live music, making it the kind of place where you can settle in, chat with locals, and feel like you're part of Red Hook's story; continue to Gowanus, where you'll find the Morbid Anatomy Library, which is a quirky, offbeat space filled with books, taxidermy, and all sorts of curiosities that explore themes of death, art, and history—it's weird in the best way and definitely something different, and end your day at Royal Palms Shuffleboard Club, where you can grab a drink and try your hand at shuffleboard in a colorful, retro setting that's all about laid-back fun and a relaxed vibe that's just right for wrapping up an unconventional Brooklyn day.

For a different slice of Brooklyn, explore Greenpoint, which combines its Polish roots with a cool, artsy energy, so start your morning at McGolrick Park, a quiet neighborhood park with a beautiful tree canopy and benches perfect for people-watching, and when you're ready for breakfast, Peter Pan Donut & Pastry Shop is where you want to be—this no-nonsense bakery serves up some of the best doughnuts in the city, so grab a coffee and a few classic glazed or jelly-filled and enjoy them like a true local, then stroll down Manhattan Avenue, lined with vintage shops, independent boutiques, and small cafes that give you that authentic, day-to-day feel of the area, and don't miss WNYC Transmitter Park, where you'll get clear, uninterrupted views of the Manhattan skyline and a bit of quiet that's hard to find elsewhere, and for a dose of local art, visit the Greenpoint Terminal Gallery, which often features up-and-coming artists and installations that reflect the neighborhood's creative pulse, and when it's time for dinner, make your way to Paulie Gee's, where you'll find wood-fired pizzas that have earned a serious reputation—try the Hellboy with hot honey, it's a game-changer, and if you're up for more, finish your night at Moonlight Mile, a laid-back whiskey bar with a friendly, down-to-earth atmosphere that makes it feel like a neighborhood hangout more than a bar, which is exactly how you want to end your Greenpoint exploration.

CHAPTER 11

BEYOND THE BASICS: SPECIAL
TIPS AND TRICKS

How to Skip the Lines: Fast Passes and Timed Tickets

I f you're looking to skip the lines and save hours, focus on booking timed tickets and fast passes for the major spots because that's your key to a smoother day without the wait—take the Statue of Liberty, for example, where the general line can eat up hours, but with a Reserve Ticket, especially if you book early for the pedestal or crown, you just breeze through security and get on the ferry with no fuss; same thing at the Empire State Building, where the Express Pass shoots you straight to the top past everyone else waiting, and even though it costs more, that extra money buys back your time, letting you enjoy the view rather than wasting it in a line that snakes around the block.

At the Metropolitan Museum of Art, skip the general admission lines with a Met Membership for fast-track access, and if museums are your thing, the City-PASS is perfect because it bundles top spots like the Met, MoMA, and the American Museum of Natural History with line-skipping privileges, so you're moving in and out with ease and hitting all the must-see exhibits without dragging your feet in endless queues; for the 9/11 Memorial Museum, a timed entry ticket is essential because those lines can stretch long and slow, but with a reserved time, you just show up, pass security, and go straight in to experience the memorial without all the waiting, and it's a similar deal at the One World Observatory where Priority Access tickets are worth it since they get you past the regular ticket line and into the elevator faster, letting you enjoy those sweeping views without delay.

Don't forget the smaller spots like the Intrepid Sea, Air & Space Museum where an Anytime Admission ticket lets you show up whenever without stressing over specific times, so if you're running late or decide to change your plans, you've got that flexibility which keeps your day flowing smoothly; same goes for places like the Central Park Zoo, where timed tickets save you from standing around especially during weekends when the crowds are heavy, meaning more time watching the animals and less time waiting to get in, and always look for mobile ticket options because these are a lifesaver, letting you skip the ticket booths entirely—just scan your phone and walk right in, and you can find these options on apps like GetYourGuide, Viator, or the attraction's own site, and many times, they even come with added benefits like special discounts or extra access that make them a no-brainer for anyone looking to cut down on wait times and maximize their experience; remember, a little planning goes a long way in a city where every minute counts, so using these tools to skip the lines isn't just about convenience, it's about making sure you're spending your time doing what you came here to do—explore, enjoy, and make the most of every moment.

Avoiding Tourist Traps

To avoid the traps that waste your time and money, skip the flashy spots that seem set up just to reel you in because they usually offer a watered-down version of the real thing—so instead of getting pulled into the overpriced chain restaurants in Times Square, head over to Hell's Kitchen just a few blocks away where you'll find authentic spots like Mercato for fresh Italian dishes or Kashkaval Garden for a cozy Mediterranean vibe with great tapas that are actually worth your money, and if you're after a slice of pizza, avoid those places with huge "best pizza" claims plastered all over the windows and head to Prince Street Pizza in Nolita or John's of Bleecker Street in the West Village where the locals go, and you'll get pizza that's famous for the right reasons, not just because it's on the tourist trail.

When you're shopping, don't waste your time in the generic souvenir shops around Midtown that charge way too much for tacky, mass-produced items—if you want something with real character, explore local markets like Artists &

Fleas in Williamsburg or Chelsea Market, where you can find unique handmade crafts, art, and food that actually feel connected to the city's creative energy, or for vintage clothing, check out Beacon's Closet where you'll dig through racks of cool finds without the hefty price tags you'd get at those overly hyped stores on Fifth Avenue, and trust me, these places are where you'll score items that people back home will actually think are cool, not just another "I <3 NY" T-shirt from a shop that looks the same on every corner.

If you're planning to visit landmarks, don't get caught up in the long lines and tourist-packed elevators at the Empire State Building—instead, go for the Top of the Rock at Rockefeller Center where the views are just as good, and you'll have the added bonus of actually seeing the Empire State Building itself in the skyline, which is exactly what you want for your photo backdrop, plus it's way less crowded and offers a smoother, quicker experience overall, or if you're near Central Park, skip the expensive and corny carriage rides and take a walk or rent a bike because you'll see way more and have a way better time exploring on your own terms without feeling like you're just part of a tourist procession, and for history and culture, pass on the cliché spots like Ripley's Believe It or Not! and opt for The Tenement Museum on the Lower East Side where you'll get real stories about immigrant life that shaped the city, or The Museum of the Moving Image in Astoria for something different that's actually engaging and unique.

When it comes to nightlife, avoid those big rooftop bars that promise stunning views but deliver overpriced drinks and wall-to-wall tourists, and try spots like 230 Fifth which has more laid-back vibes and no cover charge most nights, or check out the speakeasy scene with hidden gems like Angel's Share, tucked away behind an unmarked door in an East Village restaurant, where you get high-quality cocktails in a quiet, intimate setting that feels a world away from the typical touristy bar scene, and if you're up for exploring more, head to local hangouts like The Dead Rabbit near Wall Street for an award-winning Irish pub experience with killer cocktails, or Attaboy on Eldridge Street where the bartenders mix drinks based on your tastes—these places don't need flashy ads to pull you in because the locals already know they're worth it, and that's always the best sign that you're in the right spot.

And while you're exploring, just keep your eyes open for the obvious signs of a tourist trap: menus with photos, people hustling you on the street to come inside, or places that look too perfect are usually just set up to catch tourists, so walk a little further, dig a little deeper, and ask locals where they like to eat and hang out—most people are happy to share their favorite spots, and you'll end up with an experience that feels authentic and real, not just a quick stop on a tourist conveyor belt, so don't be afraid to step off the main roads and explore the quieter corners of neighborhoods where the real heart of the city beats because that's where you'll find the genuine experiences that make your trip unforgettable without the feeling that you've just been another tourist passing through.

Best Spots for Photos and Instagram

For those perfect Instagram shots, you'll want to go straight to Washington Street in DUMBO, Brooklyn—this is where you get that iconic view of the Manhattan Bridge framed perfectly by red-brick buildings, and you'll need to get there early, like right after sunrise, because it's a popular spot and you want that soft morning light that makes everything glow; stand in the middle of the street for the best angle, and watch for the Empire State Building peeking through the bridge's arch—it's all about getting that balance between the city's old and new, and trust me, it's a shot that never fails to impress.

If skyline views are your thing, then you need to head up to Top of the Rock at Rockefeller Center because unlike other spots, you get a full panoramic view that includes the Empire State Building itself, which is what makes the shot so special; aim for just before sunset so you can catch the golden hour turning into twilight—it's a whole vibe with the city lights flickering on as the sky goes from orange to deep blue, giving you those rich, dynamic colors that make your photos pop, and if you're in the mood for something quieter but just as stunning, check out Gantry Plaza State Park in Long Island City where the skyline looks expansive and close enough to touch, especially if you go around blue hour when the soft glow of the sky reflects off the water and makes the whole scene look almost magical without you needing to do much editing at all.

For something more green and serene, hit up Bow Bridge in Central Park—it's a classic for a reason, especially during fall when the trees are on fire with reds and oranges, and if you get a spot right on the bridge or down by the water, you can frame your shot so the city's skyscrapers just barely peek through the foliage, giving you that perfect mix of nature and urban that feels like a breath of fresh air; and while you're in the park, don't miss Bethesda Terrace where the grand staircases and the intricate tiled ceiling make for dramatic, yet peaceful photos, especially if you catch it when the light is streaming through the arcade in the morning because that's when the whole place just lights up and looks absolutely stunning.

Want a bold backdrop? Go to the Bushwick Collective in Brooklyn where the street art is massive, colorful, and always changing—just walk around and you'll find murals that cover entire buildings, each with a vibe that's unique and vibrant, making it perfect for those eye-catching shots that stand out on your feed, and if you're after that sleek, futuristic look, the Oculus at the World Trade Center offers a brilliant white interior with soaring arches that seem to glow as the sunlight pours in from above—stand in the middle or go to the upper levels for a symmetrical shot that captures the space's clean lines and impressive scale, and it's especially cool when you angle your camera to get the light beams cutting through, adding that extra touch of drama to your photos.

For architecture with a historical twist, the Flatiron Building never disappoints—grab your spot at the pedestrian triangle at 23rd Street and Broadway where you can capture the building's unique shape as it slices through the avenue, and if you're there late in the afternoon, the sunlight bouncing off the windows creates a beautiful golden reflection that adds a warm touch to your shot; and make sure to visit Grand Central Terminal because the main concourse is filled with light from those massive arched windows, and if you time it right, mid-morning light beams create those stunning rays that cut through the bustling crowd, making the whole place feel like it's alive and moving—you'll want to shoot from the balcony above the clock to get the full sweep of the hall, capturing all the energy and elegance that make this spot so iconic.

And finally, the Brooklyn Bridge is the ultimate for those sweeping shots where you're framed by the bridge's web of cables with the city spread out behind you—go early, like sunrise early, to beat the crowd and get that soft, clear light that makes everything look fresh and new, and for a different take, try shooting up through the cables or get down low to make the bridge look even more massive and grand, or take a shot halfway across where you can see both the bridge and the skyline in one frame—it's all about playing with angles and finding that perfect balance, and remember, the best photos aren't just about the view but also about capturing the moment and the feeling of standing in one of the most photogenic places in the world.

Connecting with Locals: Tours and Experiences

If you really want to connect with the city, you've got to do more than just look around—you've got to jump into experiences that put you face to face with the people who live here, so go for something like a walking tour with Big Onion Walking Tours because these aren't just guides—they're locals and historians who can tell you what really went down on these streets, not just the surface-level stuff, and you'll walk through places like the Lower East Side or Harlem, hearing about the immigrant stories, the art scenes, and how these neighborhoods became what they are today; and what's great is it's all real stories, no fluff, so you're not just seeing buildings—you're understanding the lives that built them, and that makes everything feel way more alive and connected.

For a more personal touch, try a cooking class with League of Kitchens, where you're not just following a recipe in a random kitchen—you're in someone's actual home, cooking up dishes from their homeland, and this isn't like any other cooking class because you're learning from someone who's been making these meals for years, often generations, and you're not just cooking—you're hearing stories, sharing laughs, and really getting a taste of what it means to be a part of that culture, so it's way more than just food, it's like being invited into a family, and that kind of connection sticks with you in a way that a regular restaurant meal never could, plus, the food is authentic, real, and full of flavor that you won't find in any tourist trap.

If you're into art and want to do more than just look, head to a street art workshop in Bushwick, where you'll get to see the neighborhood's incredible murals up close and then create something yourself under the guidance of a local artist, and it's not just about spraying a can—it's about understanding the stories behind the art, the struggles and the statements that these artists are making, and it's a hands-on way to engage with the creative energy of the city that's both fun and eye-opening, and trust me, there's something about leaving your own mark, even if it's just a little one, that makes you feel like you're really part of the place, not just passing through, and it's these kinds of experiences that let you see the city through the eyes of those who shape it every day.

For something that hits you right in the feels, join a Harlem Gospel Tour where you're not just listening to the music, you're feeling it—being part of a live gospel service is powerful, with the voices, the clapping, the energy in the room, and it's so much more than just a show because you're stepping into a community that's been singing these songs for generations, using music to uplift and unite, and the guides do an incredible job of making you feel welcome and explaining how gospel is woven into the fabric of the neighborhood's history, so you walk away not just having heard great music but having felt the heartbeat of the community, and that's a side of the city you can't get from just wandering around on your own.

And don't miss the chance to eat your way through the city with a food tour —think beyond just grabbing a slice of pizza or a hot dog, because there are tours that take you deep into the culinary heart of neighborhoods like Chinatown, where you'll go beyond the usual spots and into hidden gems where the locals actually eat, and it's not just about tasting amazing food like soup dumplings or scallion pancakes—it's about understanding the stories behind the dishes, the people who make them, and how food has been a way for these communities to preserve their culture and traditions, so you're getting fed in more ways than one, with a real sense of connection that sticks with you long after you've finished eating.

When you're booking, stick to platforms that specialize in local-led experiences like Airbnb Experiences or GetYourGuide—look for options where the guide is clearly someone who's lived the life they're sharing with you, not just someone reading off a script, and check the reviews to make sure you're picking something that's genuinely engaging and well-reviewed because that's your best bet for finding the tours that are more than just surface-level sightseeing— they're the ones that let you feel the pulse of the city, meet the people who make it what it is, and take home memories that feel personal and real, and booking ahead of time is key because these truly unique experiences tend to fill up fast, and you don't want to miss out on something that could be the highlight of your trip just because you waited too long to decide, so lock it in early and get ready for something that's not just a tour but a true taste of the city's soul.

Packing Like a Pro: Essentials and Extras

First thing you need to pack is a pair of comfortable walking shoes because you'll be on your feet all day—no matter where you go or what you're doing, the city is all about walking, and you want shoes that keep you moving without a second thought, and trust me, it's not worth it to try and look stylish if you're limping by midday because blisters are no joke, so go for something that's supportive and well broken-in, like your favorite pair of sneakers, and keep it simple with shoes that can handle everything from parks to sidewalks without making you regret every step, plus, if the weather's warm, breathable shoes will keep you from feeling like you're overheating before you even hit lunch.

Speaking of weather, it changes fast, so pack a lightweight, foldable rain jacket or compact umbrella because you'll thank yourself when the skies open up out of nowhere, and it's not about staying dry for the sake of it—it's about not wasting your time hiding under awnings or getting drenched between stops, and these items don't take up much space but make a huge difference in keeping your plans on track without soaking through your day, and if you're visiting in the colder months, bring a warm coat, gloves, scarf, and hat since the wind can cut right through you, especially near open spaces like parks or the waterfront, and layering is your best friend here because it keeps you warm without making you feel like you're carrying half your wardrobe with you.

For summer, you'll want to pack light, breathable clothes, sunscreen, sunglasses, and a refillable water bottle because you'll be outside a lot, and the heat can sneak up on you faster than you think, and having a water bottle means you're not constantly buying overpriced drinks when you're just trying to stay hydrated, plus most parks and many buildings have refill stations, and a small tube of sunscreen will keep you from burning up without you realizing it because the city's reflective surfaces can amplify the sun, and trust me, you don't want to spend the rest of your trip peeling or uncomfortable.

Don't forget a portable phone charger because your phone's going to be your best friend for maps, photos, restaurant finds, and everything in between, and the last thing you need is a dead battery halfway through the day when you're relying on it for everything, so a compact charger that can do at least one full charge will keep you going without hunting down an outlet in a crowded café, and also pack a secure crossbody bag or backpack with zippers to keep your essentials close and safe because it's not just about style—it's about having something functional that keeps your hands free and your stuff secure, and crowded places can be a magnet for pickpockets, so having a bag that zips up tight and stays close to your body means you're not constantly worrying about your belongings.

For those planning to bike or explore more actively, throw in a small bike lock because you don't want to get caught without one if rentals don't provide them or theirs aren't up to par, and for evenings out, have a versatile outfit that works for both day and night—something that looks good whether you're sightseeing or hitting a nicer restaurant, so you're not rushing back to change and wasting time when you could be out enjoying the city, and for little extras that can make your trip easier, pack a small first aid kit with band-aids, pain relievers, and any meds you need—just enough to cover the basics so you're not derailed by something minor like blisters or headaches.

For those into photography or just wanting to capture memories, a small, flexible tripod or selfie stick helps you get better shots without needing someone else to take your photo, especially when you're trying to get that perfect skyline pic or a group shot, and it's all about making sure you're fully prepared without feeling overloaded, so keep your packing tight, useful, and focused on items that serve multiple purposes, and you'll be ready to handle whatever the day throws at you without missing a beat.

CHAPTER 12
USEFUL RESOURCES AND APPENDICES

Important Contacts and Websites

You need the right contacts on hand to keep your trip smooth and stress-free, so first off, remember 911 for any emergencies like police, fire, or medical help—this is the number you call when things are urgent and you need immediate assistance, and for anything less pressing but still important, dial 311, which is perfect for questions about city services, reporting non-emergency issues like noise complaints, lost items, or even just to get basic info on where to find public facilities, and it's a direct line to all sorts of help without the urgency of an emergency call, so it's super handy for everyday problems or quick inquiries.

For health needs that aren't life-threatening but still need professional attention, keep Mount Sinai Hospital on your list—(212) 241-6500—because they have comprehensive emergency services and multiple locations, making it easy to get help whether it's day or night, and if you prefer having options, there's also NYU Langone Health at (646) 929-7875, which is known for excellent care and has various urgent care centers that are open late, so if something comes up that you didn't plan for, you know where to go without the stress of searching at the last minute, and for simple needs like picking up medication or health essentials, Duane Reade and CVS stores are all over the place, and most are open late or even 24 hours, so you can grab what you need without worrying about time constraints.

Navigating the city is much easier when you've got the right tools—use the MTA's official website (new.mta.info) for accurate updates on subway and bus services, including any delays, changes, or planned maintenance that might throw off your schedule, and this site is a lifesaver for planning your route before you even step out the door, and if you prefer a more mobile-friendly option, download the MTA Live Subway app, which offers the same updates but with the added convenience of real-time service alerts, detailed maps, and easy access to station info right on your phone, so you're always one step ahead and never left standing at a platform wondering what's going on.

For general navigation, you can't go wrong with Citymapper, which is more than just directions—it gives you the best ways to get anywhere whether by subway, bus, walking, or even bike-sharing, with live updates so you're not wasting time in delays or getting lost, and it's perfect for finding the quickest routes to your destinations, complete with step-by-step instructions, which is a big help when you're juggling multiple stops or need to be somewhere on time without the guesswork.

When it comes to finding things to do, places to eat, or events happening around you, the NYC Official Guide (nycgo.com) is your best bet because it's packed with the latest info on everything from special exhibits and new restaurant openings to free events and family-friendly activities, and it's a reliable source for both planning ahead and making spontaneous decisions on the go, and if you're trying to avoid the tourist traps and find more authentic spots, Yelp can be your guide with reviews and recommendations that help you choose places locals actually like, plus you get to see photos, menus, and tips from people who've been there, making it easier to pick a spot that fits what you're looking for.

For entertainment like Broadway shows, concerts, or even unique pop-up events, TodayTix and Eventbrite are your go-tos for tickets—you can score last-minute deals, see what's happening right now, and book directly from your phone without the hassle of standing in line, and these apps are easy to use, making it simple to get into the events you want without all the stress of traditional booking, plus they often have discounts that aren't available at the door, so you save time and money in one shot.

In case you ever find yourself in need of quick translations or navigating neighborhoods with diverse languages, Google Translate can handle the basics and is particularly useful for reading signs, translating menus, or even just chatting with locals when English isn't the first language, and for those times when you need a ride but don't want to deal with the unpredictability of taxis, keep Uber and Lyft ready on your phone—they're straightforward, secure, and let you choose your ride type, pay through the app, and get dropped off exactly where you need without any hassle of explaining directions, so they're a great backup for when public transport isn't the best option, and with all these resources right at your fingertips, you'll be set to handle whatever comes your way without a hitch, keeping your focus on enjoying your trip to the fullest.

Language and Phrase Guide

Alright, let's keep it straightforward—you're in the city, and getting around means understanding the lingo that locals use every day, so when someone says "Take the A train uptown," you're hopping on the A subway line going north, and these directions—uptown, downtown, crosstown—they're all about telling you which way you're headed without the fuss of too many words, so uptown is north, downtown is south, and crosstown means you're moving east to west or the other way, and that's all you really need to know to get from point A to point B without getting twisted around.

If you hear "It's a schlep," get ready for a long walk or a bit of a journey—it's just a way of saying you've got a trek ahead of you, nothing too fancy, but it's a heads-up that you might want to think twice before setting out on foot if you're short on time or energy, and when you're ordering food and someone asks "For here or to go?" just know they're checking if you want to eat in or take your meal on the go, so it's as easy as saying "to go" if you're planning to keep moving, and you'll often hear "schmear" at bagel shops—just means a spread, like cream cheese, and it's as common as coffee when you're grabbing breakfast, so don't get caught up on the terminology, just order what you want, and keep it rolling.

Locals will say "No worries" instead of "You're welcome," and it's just a casual way to keep things light and easy, and when someone asks "What's good?" they're saying "How's it going?" or "What's up?"—you can keep it simple with a "Not much" or "All good," and it's all about keeping things chill without diving into long explanations unless you're in the mood for a chat, and if someone says "That's clutch," it means something is super helpful or just what they needed in the moment, like catching a cab exactly when it starts to rain, and it's all about those little wins that make your day smoother.

For getting someone's attention in busy spots like a café or deli, use "Excuse me" or "Hey, quick question" and be direct but polite, and people here appreciate when you're straightforward—nobody's got time for beating around the bush, and if you stick around a place enough to have a go-to order, you'll hear "the usual" all the time, which is just an easy way of asking for what you always get, and while you're still finding your own spots, it's a good goal to have—feeling like you're part of the regular scene somewhere and getting to that level where you don't even need to say your order because they already know, and it's those little connections that make exploring and settling in a place so much more enjoyable.

Public Restroom Locations

If you need a restroom while exploring, head straight to the reliable spots that won't waste your time or test your patience, like Bryant Park near 42nd Street where the restrooms are always clean and well-kept, complete with attendants and even fresh flowers to make the whole experience a bit more pleasant, and they're right there next to the New York Public Library, so it's an easy stop if you're anywhere in Midtown, and don't overlook the major attractions because places like the Met, MoMA, and Grand Central Terminal offer clean facilities that are easy to find and usually have plenty of space, just remember that museum restrooms might require you to have a ticket, but they're worth using if you're already visiting because they're kept to a high standard.

When you're in the heart of Times Square, finding a good restroom can be tricky, but your best bets are large chain stores like Starbucks or McDonald's, where you can usually slip in and use the facilities without much hassle, though it can get crowded, so another option is the Times Square Visitor Center on 7th Avenue, which is a bit more of a sure thing if you're dealing with those massive crowds, and for a quieter spot, the restrooms inside department stores like Macy's at Herald Square are generally clean, tucked away near fitting rooms, and they're not as busy as you might think, making them a solid choice when you're shopping or just passing through.

If you're in the Financial District, head to the Oculus, which has some of the cleanest and most accessible restrooms you'll find in the area, right in the middle of the shops, so it's convenient and keeps you close to everything you're there to see, and the same goes for public libraries like the main branch on 42nd Street—don't be shy about walking in because their restrooms are open to the public, quieter, and generally cleaner than the average fast-food spot, so they're a great option when you need a quick and clean stop without any fuss, and they're also a good bet if you're exploring places like Bryant Park or doing a bit of sightseeing around Midtown.

And don't forget about handy apps like Sit or Squat, which can be a real lifesaver when you're out and about because it not only shows you the closest restrooms but also includes user reviews and cleanliness ratings, so you're not walking into any surprises, and this app is perfect for when you're exploring less familiar parts of the city or just don't want to waste time wandering around, plus it'll save you the trouble of guessing if a place has a restroom or if it's worth the stop, so download it ahead of time and use it to keep your day running smoothly without the stress of searching.

Accessibility Information

For accessible transportation, rely on buses because every bus in the city has ramps that fold out easily, priority seating for wheelchairs, and drivers trained to assist—you'll find stops practically everywhere, making buses the most dependable option if you're not keen on navigating the subway, and while the subway has some accessible stations, not all of them are, and it's frustrating when you run into broken elevators, so always check the MYmta app or their website, where you can filter by accessible stations, see real-time elevator statuses, and plan routes without the risk of getting stuck, especially at key locations like Times Square, Union Square, and Grand Central, where accessibility is more consistent but still requires a quick check to avoid any hiccups.

If you're looking for accessible attractions, places like the Metropolitan Museum of Art and the American Museum of Natural History have it all with ramps, elevators, tactile exhibits, and even wheelchair rentals, plus these museums offer priority entry options for guests with disabilities, making your visit smoother without the typical crowds, and when it comes to Broadway theaters, most offer accessible seating and assistive listening devices, but always double-check when booking because layouts can vary, and you want to ensure your seats meet your specific needs, especially for shows that are in high demand, and this extra step will save you from any last-minute issues when you arrive.

For accessible accommodations, most large hotels offer rooms equipped with features like roll-in showers, wider doors, and visual alarms for hearing-impaired guests, but be specific when booking—platforms like Booking.com, Expedia, and even Airbnb let you filter for exact features like step-free access, accessible bathrooms, or whatever else you need, and it's worth calling the hotel directly just to confirm, especially if your needs are very specific or if you're traveling during a busy season when room availability might be tighter, and having this confirmation gives you peace of mind so you can focus on enjoying your stay.

Navigating the streets is easier if you plan your routes around accessible crossings with audible signals and curb cuts, which you'll find in most busy areas but can sometimes be crowded or partially blocked by foot traffic, so apps like Google Maps or Wheelmap are invaluable—they offer detailed accessibility information for routes and places, showing you the best paths to take to avoid unexpected obstacles, and this can make all the difference when exploring on foot because it gives you the ability to choose the easiest routes, avoid trouble spots, and feel more confident moving through different neighborhoods, knowing that you've got all the information you need to navigate comfortably and without unnecessary detours.

CONCLUSION

You'll notice when you leave that this city sticks with you in ways you didn't expect. It's not just about the big things like the **Statue of Liberty** or the lights of **Times Square.** It's the smaller moments—the quiet walk through **Central Park** on a Sunday morning, the late-night pizza from a corner shop, or the view of the skyline as you cross the **Brooklyn Bridge** at sunset. Those are the things that will come to mind long after you've left.

You've probably felt the rush of moving with the crowd, weaving through the streets or hopping on the subway like a local, but what you'll remember most are those moments when the city slowed down for you. The way you found a hidden café, wandered into a bookstore, or stumbled upon a street performer who made you stop and listen.

There's no rush to see everything. The city is too big, too full of life to experience it all in one trip, and that's part of its charm. You'll leave knowing that there's always something new waiting for you when you come back—because even though you've seen a lot, you've only scratched the surface. There's always more to explore, and the city will always be there, changing and staying the same all at once.

Made in United States
Cleveland, OH
04 June 2025

17491992R00057